Ministering From Our Heavenly Seats

Messengers of His Kingdom
P.O. Box 833351
Richardson, TX, USA 75080
paul@messengersofhiskingdom.com

By Paul David Harrison

PNEUMATIKOS PUBLISHING
P.O. 595351
Dallas, TX 75359
www.pneumatikos.com
info@pneumatikos.com

© 2003 by Paul David Harrison

Published by Pneumatikos Publishing
P.O. Box 595351
Dallas, TX 75359
E-mail: info@pneumatikos.com
Website: www.pneumatikos.com

First printing, September 2003

Printed in the United States of America. All rights reserved under International Copyright Law. No part of this publication may be reproduced, stored in a retrieval system or transmitted in any form or by any means--for example, electronic, photocopy, recording--without the prior written permission of the publisher. The only exception is brief quotations for printed reviews.

ISBN #0-9720681-7-1

Morris Publishing
3212 E. Highway 30
Kearney, NE 68847

Cover Art Work by Fabian Arroyo

> Unless otherwise noted, scripture quotations are from the
> HOLY BIBLE, Authorized King James Version.

Dedication

*To my Heavenly Father, Almighty God
for calling me into His eternal purpose (Ephesians 3:11).*

*To my Lord Jesus Christ, Faithful and True,
for showing me how to abide (John 15).*

*To the Holy Spirit, my Teacher,
for opening the heavens to me (Ezekiel 1:1).*

Table Of Contents

INTRODUCTION		1
1	A FRESH CALL TO INTERCESSION	9
2	JOSHUA	17
3	THE ARMY CHURCH	27
4	TIME FOR TRANSITION	37
5	SEATS IN HEAVENLY PLACES	49
6	DAYS OF NOAH	63
7	PORTALS	75
8	COUNTERFEIT OF SATAN	97
9	COMMUNICATIONS IN THE HEAVENLIES	103
10	HEAVENLY TRAINING	115
11	DISCERNMENT IN THE HEAVENLIES	133
12	SENDING SPIES INTO THE LAND	145
13	A LOOK AT OUR ENEMY	153
14	ABIDING	167
15	SHAKING OF THE HEAVENS	183
RECOMMENDED READING		201

Introduction

IN MY first book, *Ministering with Angels,* I share how the Lord led me into intercession and began revealing His kingdom to me in a dynamic way. God enrolled me in the training school of the Holy Spirit, specifically teaching me how His angels will minister with believers to fulfill God's purposes in these last days.

Ministering with Angels addresses who angels really are, what they are purposed by God to do and how they operate. *Ministering from Our Heavenly Seats* begins to address the dynamics of the spirit realm and how both believers and angels operate in the heavenly realm. God is revealing to His church the need to partner with Him both in the spirit realm and the natural realm during these final hours of time as the heavens are shaken and the events prophesied in the scriptures are fulfilled.

What and How

The scriptures speak clearly of what is going to take place. God's Word is alive, and through continual revelation He is showing us how these prophecies will come to pass. For example, God promised Moses and the Children of Israel that the land was theirs and they would possess it. Possessing the land is "WHAT" God had ordained to take place.

> *And ye shall dispossess the inhabitants of the land, and dwell therein: for I have given you the land to possess it.*
> *Numbers 33:53*

"HOW" to possess the land was not revealed to Joshua until the time of possessing was to begin. Even then God led them one step at a time. He first showed Joshua how to take Jericho and then the other cities one by one.

> *And the LORD said unto Joshua, See, I have given into thine hand Jericho, ... Thus shalt thou do ... and the seventh day ye shall compass the city seven times, and the priests shall blow with the trumpets. ...and the wall of the city shall fall down flat...*
> *Joshua 6:2-5*

Throughout the scriptures we see this same pattern. The revelation of the "how" of God's ways only comes when it is time for the prophesied "what" of God's Word to be fulfilled. The same pattern is at work today. God is beginning to reveal "how" He will accomplish the great end-time events prophesied by the prophets, the apostles and our Lord Jesus Himself. In addition, the revelation of the "how" always comes to those

Introduction

seeking to know God, not to those seeking just to know what He is going to do.

Seeking the Father's Heart

Please understand me, dear reader. Our focus and desire must always remain on seeking our precious Lord. We seek to enter into His presence and to continuously develop a closer and more intimate communion with Him. Our one desire must be to seek the Father's heart.

> *One thing have I desired of the Lord, that will I seek after; that I may dwell in the house of the Lord all the days of my life, to behold the beauty of the Lord, and to enquire in his temple.*
> *Psalm 27:4*

We must abide in Him as individuals and corporately as the bride of Christ. A place of corporate abiding does exist in the Father's presence. It is in this place of intercession and abiding that the Father reveals His divine purposes and plans. It is God's intent to reveal the details of His plans before He accomplishes them. I would consider this "fresh" revelation. He has done this throughout scripture, and God declares that He will always work this way.

> *Behold, the former things are come to pass, and new things do I declare: before they spring forth I tell you of them.*
> *Isaiah 42:9*

Ministering from Our Heavenly Seats

God declared that He would not do anything without first sharing it with His servants the prophets (Amos 3:7). Jesus told His disciples that He no longer called them servants but friends. He revealed the intimate details of His purposes to those who were in constant, daily communion with Him.

> *Henceforth I call you not servants; for the servant knoweth not what his lord doeth: but I have called you friends; for all things that I have heard of my Father I have made known unto you.*
> *John 15:15*

Intercession, The Key to Revelation

God is awakening the church to the importance of prayer and intercession. They are key to our becoming God's friends and servants. Prayer and intercession, coupled with abiding in the Lord, unlocks revelation on an exponential scale. We now stand at the point in time when God is beginning to reveal the details of the last days. Man's traditional view of intercession is one where an event on earth initiates prayers toward heaven for God's intervention and mercy. God's view of intercession, true intercession, comes as the Lord stirs up individuals to pray for His purposes to be brought forth and fulfilled. Intercessors are those who are literally praying for the purposes of God to be accomplished on the earth as He reveals them from a heavenly perspective. When the Lord Jesus taught us to pray, He said, "*Thy kingdom come. Thy will be done in earth, as it is in heaven*" (Matthew 6:10).

Anna, Simeon and others were drawn by God to intercede for the first coming of Jesus. They were interceding

Introduction

not only for the birth (the inception) but also for the crucifixion (God's chosen plan) and the resurrection (the result) of Jesus' first coming.

Today intercessors are being called upon by the Lord to intercede for the climactic events of Jesus' second coming. Intercessors will see the inception of these events in the spirit realm. They will see the specifics of God's plan unveiled, as it has not been understood prior to this time. The focus of the church must not be limited to the rapture alone. It must encompass all of God's purposes for the last days. The Spirit of the Lord will release very clear revelation of the coming worldwide judgment and the events of the tribulation.

This intercession for the culmination of world events is referred to in Revelation where we find the prayers of the saints resulting in the opening of the seven seals and the blowing of the seven trumpets, each of which initiates another end-time event.

> *And when he had taken the book, the four beasts and four and twenty elders fell down before the Lamb, having every one of them harps, and golden vials full of odours, which are the prayers of saints. And they sung a new song, saying, Thou art worthy to take the book, and to open the seals thereof: for thou wast slain, and hast redeemed us to God by thy blood out of every kindred, and tongue, and people, and nation; ... And I saw when the Lamb opened one of the seals, and I heard, as it were the noise of thunder, one of the four beasts saying, Come and see.*
> *Revelation 5:8-9, 6:1*

Ministering from Our Heavenly Seats

And I saw the seven angels which stood before God; and to them were given seven trumpets. And another angel came and stood at the altar, having a golden censer; and there was given unto him much incense, that he should offer it with the prayers of all saints upon the golden altar which was before the throne. And the smoke of the incense, which came with the prayers of the saints, ascended up before God out of the angel's hand. And the angel took the censer, and filled it with fire of the altar, and cast it into the earth: and there were voices, and thunderings, and lightnings, and an earthquake. And the seven angels which had the seven trumpets prepared themselves to sound.

Revelation 8:2-6

Very pertinent to the revelation shared in this book is the shaking of the heavens that will precipitate many of these events. God is birthing intercession for the result of these climactic events, the millennial reign of Christ accompanied by His saints.

Corporate intercession and abiding allows for the releasing of continual revelation from the Throne. As God shows us specific aspects of His plans and purposes, we must agree in prayer for these prophetic events to come to pass in the perfect *kairos*[1] timing of the Lord. This corporate agreement is effective because, as Paul said, "[God] *hath raised **us up together**, and made **us sit together** in heavenly places in Christ Jesus*" (Ephesians 2:6). God is raising us up together to intercede for His purposes; not sometime in the future, but now!

Introduction

When God revealed end-time events to John the Revelator as well as other prophets, He showed them from a heavenly perspective. Most of us have an understanding of end-time events based on books and teachings that generally view the events from a limited, earthly perspective. When God revealed the insights in this book to me, He shared them from a heavenly perspective (our heavenly seats).

Roadmap for Future Encounters

This book has been written for the body of Christ, especially for intercessors, and is intended to be a roadmap. It is my prayer that by the Spirit it will help you know what to expect. Hopefully, it will enable you to interpret and understand more clearly what the Lord may reveal and require of you. Intercessors, the time has come for you to heed the call from the Father to step into your heavenly seats.

In order for you to gain the greatest benefit from reading this book, I would like to share a few things to prepare you. First of all, it would be very advantageous for you to fully read my first book, *Ministering with Angels*. It includes some foundational terms and revelations that are important for you to grasp and understand before launching into *Ministering from Our Heavenly Seats*. Secondly, you need to prayerfully ask God to prepare your heart to receive the forthcoming revelations. You need to ask the Holy Spirit to protect you from attack by any spirits of religion, tradition or criticism. These cautions should not be taken lightly. Due to the very nature of these revelations, which expose the devil, he may attack you for reading this book.

Ministering from Our Heavenly Seats

Beloved of the Father, you are about to receive many new revelations. The enemy will be vigorously trying to instill doubt and criticism. The devil does not want you to flow in the areas you are about to examine. Once again, demonic attacks may come as a result of reading this book because it exposes demonic realms and activities in places we never imagined. It is imperative that you put on the whole armor of God according to Ephesians 6 and ask our Mighty God to gird up the loins of your mind before you continue to read, *"because greater is He that is in you, than He that is in the world"* (1 John 4:4).

> *Wherefore gird up the loins of your mind, be sober, and hope to the end for the grace that is to be brought unto you at the revelation of Jesus Christ;*
>
> *1 Peter 1:13*

---

[1] *kairos*: Greek. a fixed or special occasion, i.e. set or proper time, (convenient, due) season, (due, short, while) time, a while. In contrast to *chronos*: a space of time.

1

A Fresh Call to Intercession

EVEN THOUGH the Lord has given me other giftings, I consider myself primarily an intercessor. I believe it is critical that every Christian ask God for an anointing to intercede. I have purposefully written this book from an intercessory perspective because the Lord gave me these revelations while in prayer. The Lord takes the intercessor through various seasons in their walk with Him. There are times of deep revelation and intimacy while other periods are ones of isolation and wilderness. For most of us, the ebb and flow of our individual and corporate times of intercession remains fairly consistent over time.

However, we are approaching a time of dramatic increase in the number of revelations brought forth during prayer and through our partnership with God in intercession. The purpose of this book is to prepare the church and the saints for some drastic changes in what they will experience in the spirit realm during intercession.

A Call for Corporate Intercession

I am very confident that God is calling many pastors into intercession. In order for individual churches to flow properly in the kingdom of God, its leaders must be functioning in their heavenly seats of authority. If you are a saint who desires your local church to step into a higher realm in God, then pray for your leaders! The process will always start with and flow through them. God will not move or promote a church body corporately beyond where its leaders are currently functioning in the spirit realm.

In a typical church there are individuals who move into the deeper things of the Lord and that is wonderful. However, today God is calling the entire church as a corporate body to a deeper walk with Him. God is focusing on these corporate times of intercession in order for us to receive His revelations. As a church body moves into corporate intercession, a corresponding increase in revelation will come. Corporate agreement in prayer is opening the door for unparalleled growth in revelations. This is a fresh move of God.

In our church, we as the leaders recognize that these revelations were not given to us for our own personal benefit and are an outgrowth of corporate intercession. They are intended for the body as a whole. It is not a complicated formula to follow. We have basically committed ourselves to praying corporately for hours every day through the gift of divers tongues[2]. Our purpose is first and foremost is to know the

A Fresh Call to Intercession

Lord and His ways more intimately and not to just get revelations. It has been because of our corporate passion for the Father's heart fueled by His gift for praying in divers tongues that the Lord has graciously poured forth revelation from His heart.

We usually do not pray with the understanding, but simply pray in tongues without knowing what God is praying through us. Scripture says we do not know what we ought to pray for, but the Holy Spirit does the interceding through us.

> *Likewise the Spirit also helpeth our infirmities: for we know not what we should pray for as we ought: but the Spirit itself maketh intercession for us with groanings which cannot be uttered.*
> *Romans 8:26*

As time goes on, God is giving us more insight and interpretation of what He is having us pray. The interpretation of what the Holy Spirit has been praying through us includes the revelation of what God is doing on the earth and in the heavens. Slowly but surely, the eyes of our understanding are being enlightened in the revelation of the knowledge of Him.

> *That the God of our Lord Jesus Christ, the Father of glory, may give unto you the spirit of wisdom and revelation in the knowledge of him: The eyes of your understanding being enlightened; that ye may know what is the hope of his calling, and what the riches of the glory of his inheritance in the saints,*
> *Ephesians 1:17-18*

Ministering from Our Heavenly Seats

Intercession Takes Its Rightful Place

In many churches, intercessors and prophets have been stereotyped as being "weird." It is not uncommon to hear that many of them do not get along with their pastors or other congregational members. We used to experience the same thing. However, we found that the conflicts were caused by both sides. The leadership did not recognize the importance of intercession and the prophetic, while the intercessors and prophets were usually not in submission to authority. Now we see that God is intertwining the prophetic and intercessory anointings with the pastoral leadership of the local body. As the intercessors and prophets come into submission under their pastors, their giftings will also be recognized, encouraged and developed. It is time for the church to stop being ashamed of its intercessory ministry, placing it in some remote, out-of-sight location in the church where those "weirdos" cannot embarrass the pastor or the people. If there ever was a program that should be the highlighted focus in our churches, it should be the intercessory ministry. In fact, we should see definite progress toward the intercessory ministry becoming a part of the fabric of all aspects of the church; so much so that the entire church embraces the ministry of intercession. It is the ministry of Jesus, our Chief Intercessor, and one of the ministries that the Father seeks.

> *... seeing he ever liveth to make intercession for them.*
>
> *Hebrews 7:25b*

A Fresh Call to Intercession

And I sought for a man among them, that should make up the hedge, and stand in the gap before me for the land, that I should not destroy it: but I found none.
Ezekiel 22:30

Intercession is not optional; in fact, it is the very heartbeat of God. Those in the church who are opposed to intercession should be instructed by leadership to not speak against what God is bringing forth. Gamaliel gave wise counsel to the Sanhedrin when he said,

But if it be of God, ye cannot overthrow it; lest haply ye be found even to fight against God.
Acts 5:39

There are many pastors who desire a praying church but succumb to pressures from their congregation. Unfortunately, these pastors yield to the complaints of those who threaten to leave the church or reduce their offerings and support. These pastors will answer to the Lord for not obeying what He is saying to them personally about intercession. Their church will not grow spiritually without the life and vitality that intercession brings. Spiritual growth occurs only as a church fulfills God's purposes for it in the kingdom of God. When the local church follows its own best ideas, it becomes stagnant and dull, often becoming no more than another community service organization. The local church must be more than just a place where people go to have their needs met. God has a heavenly calling for every church. He wants His church, the bride, to function in the heavenlies, in its place of authority, in order to defeat the enemies of darkness and release the glorious blessings of heaven.

Ministering from Our Heavenly Seats

Our church has stepped into a lifestyle of intercession that was designed and chosen by the Lord. We have daily times of intercession in our sanctuary, and prayer teams that intercede during many of our services. Throughout both the worship and sermon, you will often hear our intercessors praying. **Intercession can be noisy.** The noise of intercession used to bother some in the congregation, but now we find it very encouraging. Unfortunately, many left to find a place where they would not be confronted with God working through intercession in a service. The truth is, we did not get to this point of corporate unified intercession without people getting offended in one way or another. Many people were simply offended because we focused on prayer.

We are finding that God is expanding the intercession into the main service, and the people who are not "intercessors" are being drawn in by the Lord to join in this corporate intercession. If you visit our church, you will hear people praying in tongues in every service. As a result, some visitors find our services very uncomfortable and leave as soon as they can gracefully escape. We used to struggle with this, but now we do not make excuses for what God is doing among us. We certainly did not choose this way; the Lord did. We are simply obeying whatever God asks of us.

We have lost many people in our congregation because of our passion to fulfill the mandate of God to be a people of prayer and worship. Dear pastor, if you think you can follow God and keep your people happy, you are sadly mistaken. King Saul tried to do that and lost the kingdom because of it (1 Samuel 15).

The Word teaches us to pray without ceasing in order to live a life engulfed in prayer. In our church, there is a freedom for the Holy Spirit to come upon any group to intercede: Sunday school classes, worship team rehearsals, board meetings, anytime, anyplace.

Pastor / Intercessor

God is calling for pastors and leaders to receive an anointing to be bona fide intercessors. Not only does the Lord want pastors to be intercessors, He wants to train them to lead their congregations into corporate intercession. Why do pastors need to be intercessors? Paul said, *"...until Christ be formed in you"* (Galatians bbvv4:19). Jesus is the Chief Intercessor. He is calling and gifting those leaders who will follow Him in this hour with incredible intercessory anointings.

I have witnessed firsthand the fruits that are produced when pastors answer the call to the intercessory ministry of their church. My senior pastor and I not only teach the importance of prayer, but we are also vitally involved in the network of intercession in our church. We spend many hours a day in worship and intercession for the purposes of God. I intentionally did not say for the purposes of our church or our individual ministries. We pray for the things for which God directs us to pray. We do not pray from prayer lists. In fact, we pray primarily in divers tongues. Our intercession involves the negotiations of God's purposes from His Throne and His councils. We declare His purposes from heaven and come into agreement with Him for His will to be done on earth.

These are mighty days for those who will step into their heavenly authority. Jesus is calling us up into our heavenly seats. He knows the hour is short and that one of the keys to

Ministering from Our Heavenly Seats

toppling the enemy's kingdom lies in getting the saints to step into their ministry in the heavens.

---

² If you do not presently understand and operate in divers tongues, I would highly recommend reading *Divers Tongues* by Ron Crawford.

2

Joshua

BEFORE WRITING this book, the Lord led me into an in-depth study of Joshua. He wanted me to read and study the Book of Joshua with a prophetic perspective. I believe that within the Book of Joshua are many insights for what is currently taking place and will occur in the church as the coming of Christ draws near. I firmly believe we are living in the last days, and tremendous things are going to be revealed very rapidly.

The Book of Joshua focuses on the nation of Israel and their stepping into their inheritance. Joshua was called of the Lord to step into the shoes of Moses and lead the people. It was not an easy task to follow in the footsteps of a leader that had talked to God face to face, performed spectacular miracles, and been given the commandments of God for Israel. Joshua had a tough assignment.

God speaks directly to Joshua

> *...the LORD spake unto Joshua.*
> *Joshua 1:1*

The first verse in Joshua is very telling. Up until this time, God had only communicated to Joshua through Moses, but now God is speaking directly to Joshua. We do not need a mediator like Joshua had with Moses; our mediator is the Lord Jesus Christ. Jesus made a pathway to the Throne of God for believers. Now, God speaks individually to the members of the body of Christ.

> *For there is one God, and one mediator between God and men, the man Christ Jesus;*
> *1 Timothy 2:5*

God is speaking fresh words to His children. We are living in an hour where the Lord is sharing the secrets of His heart with those who commune with Him. These secrets are prophetic words to the church, and they are coming at an ever-increasing rate. It is very important to remember that God speaks to every one of His children today, not just the leaders.

The first word God gives directly to Joshua is the same message He sent to Joshua through Moses years earlier. On two different occasions in the Book of Deuteronomy, God tells Moses to encourage Joshua (Deuteronomy 1:38, 3:28). In Deuteronomy 31:7, Moses tells Joshua, in the sight of the congregation of Israel, to be strong and courageous. Then in the first chapter of Joshua, God tells him the same thing, "be strong and of good courage," four times. I asked the Lord, "Why did You have to tell Joshua the same thing so many different times?" He said that it was because Joshua had doubts and was attacked by discouragement. Joshua needed to hear this because he was not flowing in the courage that he needed to accomplish God's purposes for his life.

No Man Shall be Able to Stand Before Thee

> *There shall not any man be able to stand before thee all the days of thy life: as I was with Moses, so I will be with thee: I will not fail thee, nor forsake thee.*
> *Joshua 1:5*

What an incredible promise! Moses had been given this same promise.

> *And he shall deliver their kings into thine hand, and thou shalt destroy their name from under heaven: there shall no man be able to stand before thee, until thou have destroyed them.*
> *Deuteronomy 7:24*

Now the Lord tells Joshua that no man will be able to stand before him. This declaration reminds me of the authority that Christ has given us as believers. At Christ's resurrection, He obtained the keys of death and hell and was given all authority.

> *And Jesus came and spake unto them, saying, All power is given unto me in heaven and in earth.*
> *Matthew 28:18*

Ministering from Our Heavenly Seats

Neither Satan, fallen angels nor any man can stand up against Christ. In fact, *"every knee shall bow..."* (Philippians 2:10). Jesus has given the authority He has to His followers.

> *Behold, I give unto you power to tread on serpents and scorpions, and **over all the power of the enemy**: and nothing shall by any means hurt you.*
> *Luke 10:19*

The church, like Joshua, has been given a challenge. We must cross over into the kingdom of God to obtain our inheritance. Paul calls this inheritance *"spiritual blessings in heavenly places"* (Ephesians. 1:3). The enemy will do everything within his power to stop us from obtaining these gifts, anointings and blessings. As we walk in obedience to God, no man or spirit will be able to stand before us.

> *For I will give you a mouth and wisdom, which all your adversaries shall not be able to gainsay nor resist.*
> *Luke 21:15*

When God places a calling on your life, He will go before you, and He will also guard you from behind (Isaiah 58:8). The key to your success is your absolute obedience to His words. I am certain that Joshua had some doubts about his ability to lead such a vast host of people. He was painfully aware of the huge shoes he was filling. I am sure he felt insecure and lacking in his ability to get the job done. However, God is faithful to speak into our lives a hope for the present and for the future. The Lord sees our inability and weaknesses, but He also sees His provision for whatever we will need. **Notice how God took the burden and responsibility for Joshua's**

success and put it on His own shoulders. God promises, "*I will not fail thee....*" Here we see the abiding presence of the Lord upon Joshua. We have that same promise from Jesus when He promised us the Holy Spirit.

> *And I will pray the Father, and he shall give you another Comforter, that he may abide with you for ever;... But the Comforter, which is the Holy Ghost, whom the Father will send in my name, he shall teach you all things, and bring all things to your remembrance, whatsoever I have said unto you.*
>
> *John 14:16, 26*

When we are in God's perfect will, we do not have to carry the burden of the work of the Lord. We often go ahead of the Lord because of our impatience and fail to wait for His perfect timing.

Be Strong and of Good Courage

> *Be strong and of a good courage: for unto this people shalt thou divide for an inheritance the land, which I sware unto their fathers to give them.*
>
> *Joshua 1:6*

These words spoken by the Lord provided encouragement for Joshua right then as well as for later in his life when he would have the responsibility of dividing the land among the tribes of Israel. The Lord was telling Joshua that he would not only see the battles won over the enemy but he would also be around for the dividing of the inheritance.

Many of us receive encouragement from the Lord through His Word, a prophet or even a brother or sister in Christ. We need to write down these words and ponder them in our heart. These words will help keep us moving in the direction that God intends for us to go. They will keep our hearts from getting too heavy with the cares of this world. The apostle Paul admonishes us to keep pressing forward. It is human nature to get comfortable with where we are presently. The words spoken over us will become encouragement for us to keep pressing on.

> *I press toward the mark for the prize of the high calling of God in Christ Jesus.*
> *Philippians 3:14*

Turn Not to the Right Hand or the Left

> *Only be thou strong and very courageous, that thou mayest observe to do according to all the law, which Moses my servant commanded thee: turn not from it to the right hand or to the left, that thou mayest prosper whithersoever thou goest.*
> *Joshua 1:7*

This verse reminds us that we will also need to be strong and courageous in our commitment to obey the Lord in all things. We must be careful to pursue only the purpose of God for our lives and not envy someone else's callings and giftings. Our vision must be single and driven by the purpose of God for our lives. To be successful in the Lord, it is essential that we learn to completely focus on the path the Lord has prepared for us.

> *Thy word is a lamp unto my feet, and a light unto my path.*
> *Psalm 119:105*

> *Ye shall observe to do therefore as the LORD your God hath commanded you: ye shall not turn aside to the right hand or to the left.*
> *Deuteronomy 5:32*

As we compare Joshua 1:7 with Deuteronomy 5:32, we see that the Lord instructed Joshua in the same principles that He told Moses. It is not enough to just obey His written word, the *"logos."* We must also obey His spoken *"rhema"* word. To obey the word of the Lord means you must act on it.

> *But he answered and said, It is written, Man shall not live by bread alone, but by every word that proceedeth out of the mouth of God.*
> *Matthew 4:4*

The Lord hates lukewarmness. Jesus says in Revelation 3:16, *"So then because thou art lukewarm, and neither cold nor hot, I will spue thee out of my mouth."* He does not want a half-hearted attempt by us to obey His words, but He wants us to purpose in our hearts to obey Him. He expects complete obedience.

God is recruiting pastors and leaders for critical positions in the kingdom of God. He will be releasing a level of spiritual authority and power to His saints that this world cannot fathom.

Ministering from Our Heavenly Seats

The times ahead for leaders in the church will require strength and courage of heart. These are not positions of ease and fame, but heavenly seats of power that will battle Satan and his kingdom directly. God needs leaders like Joshua and Caleb who are 100% obedient to him.

> *Save Caleb the son of Jephunneh the Kenezite, and Joshua the son of Nun: for they have **wholly followed the Lord**.*
> *Numbers 32:12*

God is looking for leaders who will be completely committed to Him and His purposes. The tasks ahead require leaders who will forge and pioneer new trails in the spirit realm. As God permits us to see things we have never seen and to hear things we have never heard before, it is imperative that leaders of this move have an intimate relationship with the Lord and know His voice distinctly. They must listen only to Him. There will be scores of other voices telling them, "You can't do that, and you can't say that," but God wants leaders who will obediently follow His instructions no matter what.

And the Land had Rest from War

> *Until the Lord have given your brethren **rest**, as he hath given you, and they also have possessed the land which the Lord your God giveth them: then ye shall return unto the land of your possession, and enjoy it, which Moses the Lord's servant gave you on this side Jordan toward the sunrising.*
> *Joshua 1:15*

Joshua

Like Joshua, God's ultimate purpose leads the church to that "rest" which was promised to Israel. Israel was promised rest when they were obedient, had defeated their enemies and inherited their land. God purposed for Israel to find rest in Canaan. God wanted Israel to simply obey, and He would fight for them. He was teaching them to abide in His presence. It is from that place of abiding in the presence of God that they found their strength.

> *And the name of Hebron before was Kirjatharba; which Arba was a great man among the Anakims.* ***And the land had rest from war.***
> *Joshua 14:15*

Israel's inheritance or territory was a specific location here on earth. The church's inheritance or territory is to occupy our heavenly seats, which will result in the kingdom of God being manifested here on earth. Like Israel, the church will only step into God's rest when the church is obedient. We must battle and defeat the enemies who currently occupy many places of authority in the heaven in order to actually take the places Christ has prepared for us and sit in our heavenly seats. The Greek word for "high" in Ephesians 6:12 is translated "heavenly" or "celestial" in every other New Testament passage.

> *For we wrestle not against flesh and blood, but against principalities, against powers, against the rulers of the darkness of this world, against spiritual wickedness in **high** places.*
> *Ephesians 6:12*

Today Jesus still desires believers to find God's rest by abiding in Him. We will discuss "abiding" at length in chapter 14.

Ministering from Our Heavenly Seats

*I am the vine, ye are the branches: He that **abideth** in me, and I in him, the same bringeth forth much fruit: for without me ye can do nothing.*

John 15:5

3
The Army Church

> *And as soon as we had heard these things, our hearts did melt, neither did there remain any more courage in any man, because of you: for the LORD your God, he is God in heaven above, and in earth beneath.*
>
> *Joshua 2:11*

AS ISRAEL set out to battle the Canaanites, God demonstrated His astounding power as He had in Moses' day by causing the water of the Jordan to stand while the people walked across. Not only did this miracle solidify Joshua's status as leader of Israel, it also brought great fear to the people of Canaan.

A Leader Shift

In the next few years, God will raise up leaders like Joshua to lead the church to battle the kingdom of darkness. God will exhibit His awesome power and demonstrate to the enemy and this world that His anointing is upon these leaders. God is raising up leaders out of obscurity who will rapidly be launched onto the world scene. The character of these leaders will be impeccable. They will be men and women who have an intense passion for the heart of the Father and will receive their training directly from Him. He is the One to whom they will answer.

> *Paul, an apostle,* ***(not of men, neither by man, but by Jesus Christ, and God the Father****, who raised him from the dead;)*
> *Galatians 1:1*

> *For do I now persuade men, or God? or do I seek to please men? for if I yet pleased men, I should not be the servant of Christ. But I certify you, brethren, that the **gospel which was preached of me is not after man. For I neither received it of man, neither was I taught it, but by the revelation of Jesus Christ***.
> *Galatians 1:10-12*

Much like Joshua, God will be raising up men and women that *"no man will be able to stand against"* (Joshua 1:5). He is anointing His servants, and they will not fear the words of men nor give in to the pressures from organized religion. He is choosing leaders who have no hidden agendas, no political aspirations, and no hunger for power or fame. They will be humble and meek like their Lord. Their promotion will not come from any man or organization but from the Lord.

> *For promotion cometh neither from the east, nor from the west, nor from the south. But God is the judge: he putteth down one, and setteth up another.*
>
> *Psalm 75:6-7*

As I said, these men and women will have no personal agendas. Their orders will come directly from the Lord. They will be willing to die, if they must, to hold fast to the Lord and obey His words. They will not be argumentative or caustic. When they speak, people will listen because the Lord's words will abide in them (John 15:7). They know they are nothing without the Lord so they have nothing to prove or defend. They will flow in mighty and diverse ministries that will complement rather than compete with one another. This can happen only because they will have died to self and know that they should *"prefer one another"* (Romans 12:10).

These men and women will possess great authority by virtue of their preparation by the Lord. Their authority will be unique in that they will be able to adjudicate matters in the heavenlies that will have incredible impact in the places in which they minister around the world. These signs, wonders and miracles will be beyond anything the world has yet seen. They will walk in mantles and anointings similar to Elijah through whom God first declared a drought and then three and a half years later interceded for the rain (1 Kings 18). These mighty men and women will be sent by God to declare His judgment with plagues, famines and disruption of economic conditions. Like Elijah prayed for rain, they will also be sent by

God to intercede for healing, provision and deliverance in various nations around the world.

The Army Church

The Book of Joshua parallels the mandate God has given the church to move forward in spiritual warfare. Israel knew that going into the Promised Land meant they would have to fight to take the land God had promised them. Today the church faces the same challenge of stepping into her inheritance; she must fight to take the heavenly seats that God has promised to her (Ephesians 1:3, 1:20, 2:6). The church is being retooled to be an army. We will see a complete transformation of the existing church. God is calling on the church to shed peripheral ministries that tend to promote spiritual babies rather than mature warriors of God. Programs that God deems nonessential must go.

Like the illustration of the parts of the body the Apostle Paul uses in 1 Corinthians 12, each church will have different functions. Christ is the head of the body, and each church must answer to Him independently. Even though churches will have different callings, there will be unity and an ability to work together in harmony because the Holy Spirit is in charge.

God's church is not a civilian church. It is an army church. Everyone must stay in his or her rank and obey those in leadership over them. In the army, soldiers that do not obey do not get promoted, and those who do not show up for their duty are reprimanded. If they leave without permission, they are considered AWOL and are disciplined accordingly. Soldiers that continually disobey are court-marshaled. Those that cannot handle the military environment go back to civilian life. This is how it is going to be for the end-time church. The church is the bride, but it is also an army.

> *Who is she that looketh forth as the morning, fair as the moon, clear as the sun, and terrible as an army with banners?*
>
> Song of Solomon 6:10

Watchman Nee's book, *The Normal Christian Church*,[3] describes how the government of the church should operate based on the New Testament pattern. I suggest you read it. Basically, Nee teaches that every church should answer directly to the Lord for its direction. Nee did not have much use for the denominational structure of the present day church. He felt denominations fostered division and exclusivity.

It is not surprising that churches should have very different callings. Like the military, there are multiple branches of service with each having distinguishing responsibilities. Even though job responsibilities and technical expertise are drastically different in each branch, they come together and blend their expertise to fight as one mighty force. Churches were never intended to be "cookie cutter" products of massive denominations. They were created to function as the body of Christ; their main purpose being to minister to the Lord and then to fulfill His purposes as He reveals them for each specific community.

The Neutered Church

There are some very important messages that God wants to communicate to His churches and their leaders. He does not care about the size of the congregation, nor how many programs or ministries are operating within the church. In fact, if God had His way, He would probably shut down 90% of our churches and start over. Most churches have been neutered by the enemy and have become spiritually ineffective in their communities, cities and states. God is tired of hearing prideful churches proclaim their grandeur. They may appear to be very beautiful and successful, but unfortunately most of the people who attend them have their own interests at heart and are not seeking or following the Lord.

What can we do with this widespread problem within our churches? Every church member would do well to join with their pastors and leaders and take a month to dedicate themselves to nothing but fasting and prayer for God's mercy and His guidance. It is time for the church to turn to divine means of direction instead of relying on man's wisdom. The Lord has taught me to commit myself to waiting on Him for what my next move needs to be, even if it means not knowing where the money will come from for ministry or family expenses. When a decision needs to be made in our church or questions arise about what we are to do, we go before the Lord. Our board prays for guidance and truly seeks God for the answer, which may come in the form of dreams, visions or prophetic insight. I am so grateful for the church in which God has placed me. We are all committed to the same purpose, which is moving only as directed by the voice of the Holy Spirit.

The Army Church

As I said earlier, the church will become an army. My hope as I share these revelations the Lord has given me is that you will realize the nearness of the hour of the Lord's return. The saints will be pitted against incredible demonic powers. God is in the process of preparing us for these confrontations; otherwise, we will be utterly defeated.

> *With him is an arm of flesh; but with us is the LORD our God to help us, and to fight our battles. And the people rested themselves upon the words of Hezekiah king of Judah.*
> *2 Chronicles 32:8*

> *Therefore the LORD left those nations, without driving them out hastily; neither delivered he them into the hand of Joshua. ... Only that the generations of the children of Israel might know, to teach them war, at the least such as before knew nothing thereof; ... And they were to prove Israel by them, to know whether they would hearken unto the commandments of the LORD, which he commanded their fathers by the hand of Moses.*
> *Judges 2:23, 3:2, 4*

Jesus, The Captain of the Lord's Host

> *And he said, Nay; but as captain of the host of the Lord am I now come. And Joshua fell on his face to the earth, and **did worship**, and said unto him, What saith my lord unto his servant? And the captain of the Lord's host said unto Joshua,*

Ministering from Our Heavenly Seats

> *Loose thy shoe from off thy foot; for the place whereon thou standest is holy. And Joshua did so*
> *Joshua 5:14-15*

Many people do not understand that Jesus is still the captain of the Lord's host and He is coming to battle. He died for our sins, but He lives as a victorious warrior who will lead His church, His army, in battle against the hosts of hell.

Joshua received an unprecedented visitation of the Lord Himself just like the church is about to experience. When Jesus comes on the scene, He is accompanied by His angels. As I shared in my first book, there will be the most incredible encounters with angels the world has ever witnessed. Why is that? Jesus is the *"captain of the host of the Lord"* and He leads an army of countless, well-trained angels. When Jesus is in the midst, there is always an increase in angelic activity.

There is a debate about the identity of who this "captain" really was, but I think it is very clear. We know from scripture that the angels of the Lord will not allow anyone to worship them, and Joshua 5:14 says very clearly that Joshua worshipped this being (the captain of the Lord's host). Since Joshua worshipped this being, we know this was a visitation from the Lord.

> *For thou shalt worship no other god: for the Lord, whose name is Jealous, is a jealous God:*
> *Exodus 34:14*

When Jesus came to visit Joshua, His purpose was to encourage and to assure Joshua that he would not be fighting alone – nor will we. The Lord and His angels are making visitations all over the world to prepare the church for the nearing confrontations with the enemy. Just as the Lord had His sword drawn when He encountered Joshua, the Lord is readying His sword in this hour as well. The Lord is coming to fight, and His church had better wake up to the news.

---

[3] Watchman Nee, *The Normal Christian Church Life*, (Anaheim: Living Stream Ministry, 1994).

Ministering from Our Heavenly Seats

4 Time for Transition

Pass through the host, and command the people, saying, Prepare you victuals; for within three days ye shall pass over this Jordan, to go in to possess the land, which the LORD your God giveth you to possess it.

Joshua 1:11

AFTER BEING in the wilderness for forty years with God as the sole provider of their needs, Joshua announced to the officers that they needed to prepare victuals (food, meat, or provision) for the impending crossing of the Jordan River. God was preparing them to take some responsibility for their own welfare. Why? Because within a few days their daily supply of manna would cease. Not only was there a transition in leadership, there was also a transition in provision. The Lord was not ceasing to provide for them, but was transitioning them from being dependent children into mighty warriors. They would have to trust God for their safety and success. We all must go through transition during our walk with the Lord. I went from being incredibly busy in ministry to spending several years where I just sought the Lord in prayer and studied. Today the Lord has transitioned me back into the work of the ministry, and I use the prayer and study habits the Lord taught me to fuel the work God has called me to do.

In many ways Joshua's announcement of the manna provision ceasing *"within three days"* was a "suddenly" of the Lord. After forty years of wandering in the desert, Moses, their beloved leader, was dead. In addition, their daily provisions were about to cease, and a declaration of war on Canaan was imminent. We must learn to flow with God's "suddenlies." If not, we will not stay on the cutting edge of what God is doing! The Spirit of the Lord is not predictable, in fact, He moves when and where He wants. To keep up with Him, we must obey His voice and flow with His suddenlies.

> *The wind bloweth where it listeth, and thou hearest the sound thereof, but canst not tell whence it cometh, and whither it goeth: so is every one that is born of the Spirit.*
> *John 3:8*

Preparation

> *Pass through the host, and command the people, saying, Prepare ...*
> *Joshua 1:11*

During the transitional times in our churches and in our personal walk with the Lord, there are always seasons of preparation. God puts us in boot camp to get us ready for the next move of His Spirit. Moses, David, John the Baptist, Jesus, Paul and many others all spent time in the Lord's boot camp. They were preparing for their assignments. God wants us moving and growing in Him, and He is always preparing us to move from "glory to glory" (2 Corinthians 3:18).

The Lord wanted Israel to move into a deeper trust in Him. He took away their daily provision, which caused their faith to be tested. Israel would have to believe that God would provide for their daily sustenance in a different way than the way in which they had become accustomed. God was taking them from supernatural provision for their food to a place of supernatural provision for their safety and victory over their enemies. God would still be moving in their lives supernaturally, but it would not be manifested so predictably or as often in the natural. This was the only way for Israel to grow up in their faith in God. They had not lost favor with God; rather He was helping to strengthen their faith by giving them the responsibility for securing their own victuals and no longer providing manna on a daily basis. In essence, He was teaching them to exercise faith in order to experience greater realms of His provision. God had given Joshua and the children of Israel great vision and purpose. As they actually stepped into the fulfillment of their prophetic words, the foundation of faith in Him was being built.

> *Moses my servant is dead; now therefore arise, go over this Jordan, thou, and all this people, unto the land which I do give to them, even to the children of Israel.* ***Every place that the sole of your foot shall tread upon, that have I given***

> **unto you**, *as I said unto Moses. From the wilderness and this Lebanon even unto the great river, the river Euphrates, all the land of the Hittites, and unto the great sea toward the going down of the sun, shall be your coast.*
>
> *Joshua 1:2-4*

God was literally establishing them in a new place in Him. When you step into a new dimension of the Lord, you must have total trust in Him.

Provision

> *This is that bread which came down from heaven: not as your fathers did eat manna, and are dead: he that eateth of this bread shall live for ever.*
>
> *John 6:58*

We know from scripture that Jesus is the Living Word (John 1:1) and the Bread of Life (John 6:35). For forty years the nation of Israel had survived on manna, which is a type of bread. Basically, Israel was established on Christ as the Word, symbolized by the manna. However, God did not want them to continue being satisfied with this level of knowing Him. He wanted them to be established in a new form of provision.

> *Therefore leaving the principles of the doctrine of Christ, let us go on unto perfection; not laying again the foundation of repentance from dead works, and of faith toward God,*
>
> *Hebrews 6:1*

As they moved to this next level of provision or establishment, the provision would be manifested as a sword instead of manna. Both the bread and the sword are symbolic of Christ, but they represent different levels of spiritual maturity.

> *But he answered and said, It is written, Man shall not live by bread (manna) alone, but by every word (sword) that proceedeth out of the mouth of God.*
>
> *Matthew 4:4*

In this hour, God is calling the body of Christ to move from living solely on the provision of bread (manna) to being established, both individually and corporately, in the sword of Christ. We must believe God for fresh revelations and *rhema* words. During Israel's journey in the wilderness, even though they were sustained by the manna sent from heaven, they still had many spiritual shortcomings. It was a:

- Time of barrenness and ineffectiveness
- Time of murmuring and complaining
- Season of knowing of the promises of God but inability to step into them
- Setting for rebellion which led to conflict among its leaders and people
- Time of no direction (they went in circles) – no discernment
- Time of no spiritual growth, no new revelations of God's provision

- ❖ Time when they had the Law, but not the power

- ❖ Time when they could win a battle, but they did not have the anointing to take the land, YET.

At our church, we have had an abundance of revelation; however, our provisions have seemingly all but dried up. We have had to live by faith for our provision. It has been worth it because the provision of the sword brings incredible revelation of His purposes. God takes you from a dependence on natural provision to a reliance on supernatural provision. If you take the pathway of the sword of Christ, you must be ready for major changes and challenges in your life, your family and your church. The incredible price to pay to step into supernatural provision is dying daily to the flesh.

Establishment of the Sword

> *And it came to pass, when Joshua was by Jericho, that he lifted up his eyes and looked, and, behold, there stood a man over against him with his sword drawn in his hand: and Joshua went unto him, and said unto him, Art thou for us, or for our adversaries? And he said, Nay; but as captain of the host of the LORD am I now come.*
> *Joshua 5:13-14a*

When Israel fought with the Amalekites (Exodus 17), the victory came through the **intercession of Moses** and by the **edge of Joshua's sword**. God told Moses to remind Joshua again and again about this day. Why? It was not for that generation's benefit, but for the next one, which would flow in God's next establishment of provision. We see from this passage that **intercession is a key to unlocking the power and establishment of the sword**.

When the Captain of the Lord's host came to Joshua, He brought a fresh revelation of how God wanted the people of Israel to fight their enemies and take the Promised Land. It is the same in the church when the sword is established; it ushers in a new revelation about how God wants His people to move and battle in spiritual warfare. The Word as the sword brings us into direct confrontation with the enemy of our souls. This requires the Living Word (Jesus, the Captain of the Lord's host) to teach us to use His sword, which is fresh revelation, to battle the enemy. Revelation is a powerful weapon in the spirit realm. The Book of Revelation depicts Jesus as having a two-edged sword coming out of His mouth, and in Hebrews it speaks of the Word being sharper than a two-edged sword.

> *For the word of God is quick, and powerful, and sharper than any twoedged sword, piercing even to the dividing asunder of soul and spirit, and of the joints and marrow, and is a discerner of the thoughts and intents of the heart.*
> *Hebrews 4:12*

> *And he had in his right hand seven stars: and out of his mouth went a sharp twoedged sword: and his countenance was as the sun shineth in his strength.*
> *Revelation 1:16*

As far as we know, Moses had not received this revelation of the Captain of the Lord's host. With the exception of Joshua and Caleb, the leaders and people of Israel who had seen God's power but did not follow His ways were not allowed to enter into the Promised Land nor experience God's new provision. How can we relate this to the church today? Like Israel, the church demonstrates many of the same shortcomings.

- ❖ Barren and ineffective

- ❖ Complaining and murmuring about one another, their leaders, and their country

- ❖ Aware of its future inheritance but unable to step into it

- ❖ Rebellious and in conflict within and between churches

- ❖ Lacks direction and discernment

- ❖ Little spiritual growth and less numerical growth than is claimed

- ❖ Knows the Word, but lacks the power

- ❖ Wins occasional battles, but the land is firmly held in the grasp of the kingdom of Satan, FOR NOW.

Fruit of Revelation

God wants the body of Christ to move from the provision of manna to the establishment of the sword. What can happen during the establishment of the sword (revelation)? Here again we look to the Book of Joshua for some answers:

Time for Transition

- Promotion (1:2)

- Fulfillment of prophetic words (1:2)

- Come into your inheritance (1:2)

- Complete victory over your enemies (1:3)

- No man able to stand before you (1:5)

- Promise of an abiding presence of the Lord (1:5)

- Promise of success (1:7)

- Revelation of the Word of God (1:8)

- Freedom from fear and discouragement (1:9)

- Submission and cooperation of the people with their leaders (1:16-17)

- No rebellion allowed (1:18); see Achan's sin (7:1)

- Strange spiritual warfare (6:3-5)

- Supernatural victories (6:20)

- High standard of holy living (5:2); circumcised the males and judgment for Achan's sin (7:24-25). The word "knives" in Joshua 5:2 is the same Hebrew word used for "sword" in other Joshua passages.

- Ambushing of the enemy (8:7)

- Renewing of the covenant (8:32)

- ❖ Deceitfulness of the enemy is increased (9:1-27); the people of Gibeon remind us of false Christs, false prophets, false apostles, false teachers.

- ❖ The Lord fights for you (10:10-11); "the Lord discomfited and slew them," "the Lord cast down great stones from heaven...."

- ❖ If needed, God will stop time (11:13-14)

- ❖ God will destroy the enemy's weapons (11:6); "burn their chariots"

- ❖ The Lord will send the enemy to be defeated by us (11:20)

- ❖ We will destroy the "giants" (12:21-22); demonic warriors

- ❖ We will defeat the kings (12:7-24); demonic princes and authorities; thirty-one kings were defeated fulfilling the Abrahamic covenant

- ❖ Individual inheritances given (13:1-33)

- ❖ Possess and dwell in our inheritance (21:43-45)

- ❖ One man chased a 1000 (23:10); (Isaiah 30:17, Isaiah 60:22)

- ❖ Obedience is the key to having favor with God (23:16)

- ❖ Sides are chosen (24:15)

Typically, believers think of the sword as indicative of spiritual warfare; however, the Lord recently shared with me that swords often represent new revelations. On many occasions over the last several years, the Lord has given me various kinds of swords. Once while I was in intercession, He put a stack of swords in my arms and said they were to be given to other saints. A few weeks later, the Lord had me distribute them during a ministry time in one of our services. The swords symbolize a season of tremendous new revelations coming to the church.

Revelation comes through the sword, not through the manna. Manna was provided for a season, and then it stopped. You cannot survive in these last days on a steady diet of manna. You must be established in the sword. We must be pressing into the heart of the Lord to receive fresh revelation from Him for the times in which we are living. The scriptures teach us to listen to every word that God speaks; He did not stop speaking when He closed the cannon of scripture. It is imperative that we continue to listen to what God is saying.

> *But he answered and said, It is written, Man shall not live by bread alone,* ***but by every word that proceedeth out of the mouth of God****.*
> *Matthew 4:4*

Jesus taught a series of parables about the kingdom of heaven; the kingdom of heaven was like a treasure and like a pearl that the finder would sell everything to possess. Treasures and pearls in scripture often refer to wisdom, which must be sought for and brought to light or revealed. Jesus concludes the parables by explaining to His disciples in private that these treasures of wisdom are like a householder who brings forth both "old" (already known wisdom) and "new" (fresh revelation) out of his storehouse.

> *Then said he unto them, Therefore every scribe which is instructed unto the kingdom of heaven is like unto a man that is an householder, which **bringeth forth out of his treasure things new and old**.*
> *Matthew 13:52*

> *So that thou incline thine ear unto wisdom, and apply thine heart to understanding; Yea, if thou criest after knowledge, and liftest up thy voice for understanding; **If thou seekest her as silver, and searchest for her as for hid treasures**;*
> *Proverbs 2:2-4*

> *In whom are hid all the treasures of wisdom and knowledge.*
> *Colossians 2:3*

It is also important that the fresh revelation lines up with the scriptures. We must be like the Bereans who were eager to receive the prophetic word but searched the scriptures to verify the words were true.

> *These were more noble than those in Thessalonica, in that they received the word with all readiness of mind, and searched the scriptures daily, whether those things were so.*
> *Acts 17:11*

Seats in Heavenly Places

*Blessed be the God and Father of our Lord Jesus Christ, who hath blessed us with all spiritual blessings **in heavenly places** in Christ:*
Ephesians 1:3

*Which he wrought in Christ, when he raised him from the dead, and set him at his own right hand **in the heavenly places**,*
Ephesians 1:20

*And hath raised us up together, and **made us sit together in heavenly places** in Christ Jesus:*
Ephesians 2:6

Ministering from Our Heavenly Seats

> *To the intent that now unto the principalities and powers **in heavenly places might be known by the church** the manifold wisdom of God,*
> *Ephesians 3:10*

Heavenly Seats

THE WORD of God establishes that there are heavenly seats, and they are ruled over by our Lord Jesus Christ. There is also a clear calling for those who love and know Him to step into these seats. These places in the heavenlies are places of leadership and authority. Many of them are supply points for spiritual revelations and unique anointings. These places in the heavenlies represent our inheritance.

There has not been a lot of teaching along these lines. In fact, most Christians expect they must wait until they die and go to heaven before they claim their inheritance. Satan loves to see believers waiting to receive their inheritances in the afterlife. He knows those believers are little threat to his kingdom. Therefore, he mobilizes against the saints who are presently functioning in their heavenly seats. These saints find themselves constantly under the surveillance and attack of the enemy.

We have established that there is an inheritance, which God wants His children to attain. Our Promised Land is in the heavenly places. To receive our inheritance requires a lifestyle of intercession and holy living. Once we are operating in these heavenly places, we will begin receiving fresh revelation as to the purposes of God both individually and corporately. These revelations will include strategies on how to remove demonic forces that currently occupy many places of spiritual authority.

In order for Israel to occupy Canaan and be given their inheritance, they had to fight with the enemy. God would intervene many times during their battles, but He also expected them to do their part. The Lord fights for us, but He also expects us to intercede and engage in whatever spiritual warfare He deems necessary. God always partners with His people.

> *Wherefore, holy brethren, **partakers** of the heavenly calling, consider the Apostle and High Priest of our profession, Christ Jesus;*
>
> *Hebrews 3:1*

> *Giving thanks unto the Father, which hath made us meet to be **partakers** of the inheritance of the saints in light:*
>
> *Colossians 1:12*

From a study of the Greek, the word "partakers" in these scriptures means participant or partner. In other words, we are being asked of the Lord to participate with Him in the heavens.

In our study of Joshua, the first battle to take place under his leadership was with Jericho. Before the battle took place Joshua had an encounter with Jesus and received his battle plans. In addition, Joshua sent two spies to check out what was going on in Jericho. God miraculously protected the spies while they carried out their mission. These two spies had a completely different viewpoint of potential victory than most of the original spies that Moses sent out.

> *And they said unto Joshua, Truly the LORD hath delivered into our hands all the land; for even all the inhabitants of the country do faint because of us.*
> *Joshua 2:24*

Spying out Our Inheritance

The Lord is sending forth His saints to spy out the land of their inheritance. Remember our inheritance is in heavenly places in Christ Jesus. Our response to being sent out as spies is very critical. The saints will encounter many shocking things in the heavenlies. Some may even shy back and refuse to move into these realms of the spirit. However, we cannot be like the ten spies who had no faith and allowed the giants in the land to instill fear in their hearts.

There are some fearful sights out in the heavenlies. There are many "giants" in the dark kingdom who are poised to fight and resist our offensive maneuvers. The enemy has enjoyed the places he occupies, and the giftings he has stolen. You must realize that the enemy will most certainly resist any force that might try to remove him.

Many saints will soon be moving into the realms of authority that the Lord intended for them. As a result, we will see an unprecedented manifestation of spiritual authority to destroy the strongholds of the enemy. In taking back our cities and nations for the kingdom of God, this authority will enable us to deal directly with the principalities and dominions in high places that control cities and nations. The Lord is going to show Himself mighty! He is going to defeat the enemy at every point. Jesus Christ did everything that was legally necessary to defeat the enemy once and for all. The Lord is tired of the enemy ruling and reigning in places where he does not belong. These places were secured by the Lord Jesus Christ and are destined to be populated and ruled by His children.

The Meat of the Word

> *Who then is a faithful and wise servant, whom his lord hath made ruler over his household, to give them meat in due season?*
> *Matthew 24:45*

Could this verse be talking about our heavenly place in Christ; and if so, could this be the meat of the Word or the deeper revelations of Christ?

It is so crucial for believers to take their seats in heavenly places. We need the authority that comes to those who advance into these places. We need to take back from the enemy all the gifts that he has absconded from places that God's children never occupied. These places belong to us.

> *Then shall the King say unto them on his right hand, Come, ye blessed of my Father, inherit the kingdom prepared for you from the foundation of the world:*
> *Matthew 25:34*

> *That ye be not slothful, but followers of them who through faith and patience inherit the promises.*
> *Hebrews 6:12*

Satan has a right to his first estate, but unfortunately he rules from many of our heavenly places, too!

> *For the gifts and calling of God are without repentance.*
> *Romans 11:29*

Does this mean that we can take back from the enemy gifts forfeited by believers that do not use them? It seems to me that anything the enemy can steal, we can take back. I believe the power of the cross provides us with the authority to do so.

> *... and they shall spoil those that spoiled them, and rob those that robbed them, saith the Lord GOD.*
> *Ezekiel 39:10b*

> *Therefore all they that devour thee shall be devoured; and all thine adversaries, every one of them, shall go into captivity; and **they that spoil thee shall be a spoil, and all that prey upon thee will I give for a prey.***
> *Jeremiah 30:16*

Satan Fears Our Intimacy with the Lord

Satan knows that intimacy or abiding in the Lord and intercession are the most powerful weapons of the believer. However, Satan wants believers to think that his own power is very limited. It is without question that God in His sovereignty is immensely more powerful than Satan. Christians falsely assume they have more power than the demonic realm as well.

They do not realize that they are not ready to deal with the demonic powers in heavenly places until they have been brought into the appropriate level of authority in Christ Jesus.

Christians that go to church and read their Bibles do not bother the devil too much. Being a great soul winner or having your own ministry does not necessarily qualify you for greater authority in the spirit realm. Satan knows his greatest threat comes from those Christians who walk intimately with the Lord in the spirit realm. This walk can be closely related to a pilgrimage. It is the process by which we come to truly know the Father's heart. As a result of that pursuit, we receive gifts, anointings, and eventually authority from our Father. The Lord determines through relationship and obedience the measure of authority with which we can be entrusted. Satan wants believers to think that the knowledge of scripture alone brings authority.

As we fight and overcome demonic forces in the spirit realm, we receive even greater authority. In God's perfect timing, this authority will be manifested on earth and will make the difference between an occasional healing and thousands being healed at once.

Step into Your Inheritance Now

There is yet another deception of the enemy. Satan constantly tries to keep believers from realizing their inheritance presently awaits them. The enemy keeps us busy chasing after the attainments that can come to us in the here and now on earth. We sing about the "Sweet Bye and Bye" without realizing that God has our inheritance just waiting for us to receive now. When we get saved, we are born again in the Spirit. We are

God's children and now have the ability to begin receiving the heavenly treasures and gifts that have been acquired for us by Christ's life, death and resurrection. Oh, what an inheritance! Believers are missing out on what God has planned for them by failing to move into the land He has prepared for them. We are living our Christian lives outside the Promised Land and pose no threat to the enemy until we enter.

Heavenly Standards are High Standards

Although the demands on saints will be greater in the heavenlies, the giftings are mightier, too. The responsibility to fall under authority is absolutely essential. Upon stepping into the heavenlies, the standard for obeying orders and the Lord's commands are lifted higher. Those things that once caused us to stumble and drift from the Lord cannot be allowed to influence us anymore.

> *... For unto whomsoever much is given, of him shall be much required: and to whom men have committed much, of him they will ask the more.*
> *Luke 12:48b*

When operating in the spirit realm, we represent the Lord. We are His ambassadors. As ambassadors, we speak only what the Father tells us to say. Our personal opinions should have no influence on what we do or say. We must follow God's agenda, not ours. We must do only what the Lord says to do and nothing more. Do not get frustrated when you are asked to do things without having a clue as to what you are really accomplishing. My dear friend, that is what it is like to *"...walk by faith, not by sight"* (2 Corinthians 5:7).

When the Lord gives you a specific task or mission to accomplish, alternative tasks or objectives often will present themselves. We must not be sidetracked and pursue targets that are not specifically commanded by the Lord. For example, the Lord may have you praying in divers tongues and declaring His will from a heavenly council, when suddenly a demonic being will appear. Only if the Lord directs you to confront the demon, should you divert your focus from the assigned task of declaring the Lord's will. Remember the enemy's strategy is to distract and derail the purposes of God. He wants to get you off course.

> *Ye shall observe to do therefore as the LORD your God hath commanded you: ye shall not turn aside to the right hand or to the left.*
> *Deuteronomy 5:32*

Councils in Heaven

We may be limited in our intelligence and abilities here on earth; however, through our Lord Jesus Christ we do incredible things in the heavens. I have been amazed at the heavenly places into which God has taken me to minister. As the Lord takes your spirit into heaven, be prepared for an incredible amount of activity. The Word says, *"For our conversation is in heaven; from whence also we look for the Saviour, the Lord Jesus Christ"* (Philippians 3:20). We should be more attuned to the spirit realm than we are to this world.

Ministering from Our Heavenly Seats

The Lord has brought me into alignment with His purposes. In the early revelations that I was given by the Lord, my intercession was almost entirely about things on the earth. Now, a larger percentage of my time is spent making declarations on behalf of the Lord's purposes for the heavenlies. Individually, we all must be in alignment with God's purposes for us, which He established from the foundation of the world. Every believer must line up with God's purpose for them.

> *According as he hath chosen us in him before the foundation of the world, that we should be holy and without blame before him in love:*
> *Ephesians 1:4*

All of us are called to take our heavenly seats and to intercede from that heavenly perspective. You can look forward to doing His bidding in various places throughout the heavens, especially in the second heaven. Sometimes you will be assigned to intercede for God's purposes in the heavens, while at other times you will be assigned to intercede for God's purposes for the earth.

God is calling His saints up into the heavens for many reasons. One reason is to sit on the many councils that are in heaven. God loves to bring His people together in order to come into agreement with His purposes. He always operates according to His Word and thus He brings together a multitude of counselors for His purposes just as He instructed us in Proverbs.

> *Where no counsel is, the people fall: but in the multitude of counsellors there is safety.*
> *Proverbs 11:14*

Seats in Heavenly Places

*And hath raised us up together, and made us **sit together in heavenly places** in Christ Jesus:*
Ephesians 2:6

It is so awesome that God gives us the honor of representing Him on these councils and allows us to speak forth His words of wisdom. These councils are made up of saints that are both on earth and those in heaven, angels and various other heavenly beings. As saints, we are literally representatives of the Lord Himself on these councils. He speaks through us. *"If ye abide in Me and My words abide in you..."* (John 15:7).

God wants His children ministering from the heavens. You will find you are as comfortable doing things in the heavens as you are here on earth. The Lord frequently has me sitting on heavenly councils and declaring His purposes in tongues. You may not always understand what is being discussed at these councils; nevertheless, the Lord wants to place you there to declare His purposes. Prophetic words that are issued forth from these councils will in time be fulfilled on the earth. We are called to be Christ's ambassadors, not speaking our own thoughts or words, but only His.

Now then we are ambassadors for Christ,...
2 Corinthians 5:20

Eventually, many saints will find themselves on one of these heavenly councils. Do not let the enemy trap you with pride or false humility. Pride would lead you to believe that your own endeavors have brought you a promotion into sitting on a heavenly council. Paul reminds us that God chooses the weak and foolish to do His works. False humility is the opposite but equally effective strategy of the enemy that causes us to think we could never be used by God in a place of such import.

Ministering from Our Heavenly Seats

> *But God hath chosen the foolish things of the world to confound the wise; and God hath chosen the weak things of the world to confound the things which are mighty;*
>
> *1 Corinthians 1:27*

As you abandon yourself and take steps of faith, you will be amazed at how the Lord will use you. He will reveal to you things about Himself and the heavens that you never imagined. They are truly the things that *"eye hath not seen, nor ear heard"* (1 Corinthians 2:9).

You may be handed scroll-like documents to read while sitting on these councils. At other times, the Spirit will come upon you to declare something for Him or simply to stand in agreement for His purposes. If nothing else, it is great to just listen to the unique way the various members of the council express themselves. I love the fact that God does not do everything Himself, but loves to have His children and the angels partner together with Him for His purposes. Everything that is said and done in these councils is completely sanctioned and overseen by the Father. It is vital that the saints begin to take their heavenly seats and allow the Lord to teach and show them what their responsibilities are in heaven.

Councils in the Dark Realm

It is very interesting that there are also councils in the dark realm (Psalm 1). The enemy declares his purposes from the heavens as well. He has human souls who have reached certain authority levels in the kingdom of darkness and fallen angels sitting on his councils.

*Hide me from the secret counsel of the wicked;
from the insurrection of the workers of iniquity.*
Psalm 64:2

Some intercessors will become spies in the enemy's territory. Many times the Lord hides you and allows you to listen to the strategies of the enemy without his knowledge. This has happened to many intercessors. They have been able to pray and stop the enemy because God allowed them to discover the enemy's plans.

Ministering from Our Heavenly Seats

Days of Noah

AS THE Lord allows you to enter the second heavens, you may see many beings from the kingdom of darkness. An understanding of who inhabits Satan's kingdom might be very helpful at this point. In the gospels, Jesus gave us prophetic insight about the characteristics of the end-times, one of which is a reference to the days of Noah.

> *But as the days of Noe were, so shall also the coming of the Son of man be.*
> *Matthew 24:37*

To find out what those days were like, you would need to study Genesis chapters 4 to 7. I am not going to give a complete analysis of all the information contained in these chapters, but I will highlight **one** aspect of what was transpiring during the time of Noah. I am being very specific because the revelations I have received focus primarily on one particular area – the second heaven.

It is very crucial that you understand the basic framework I will be using to discuss the time of Noah and its connection to the heavenlies. I am by no means an expert on this subject, but I believe the Lord has shown others and myself through scripture and divine revelation enough to give a brief explanation. Personally, I have benefited greatly from the glimpses the Lord has given even though I still only *"know in part"* (1 Corinthians 13:9).

Sons of God

To begin our quest, let us look at Genesis 6:

*That the **sons of God** saw the daughters of men that they were fair; and they took them wives of all which they chose.*
Genesis 6:2

*There were giants in the earth in those days; and also after that, when the **sons of God** came in unto the daughters of men, and they bare children to them, the same became mighty men which were of old, men of renown.*
Genesis 6:4

Who are these "sons of God?" I am not sure whether these "sons of God" is a classification of angels, perhaps high-ranking ones, or if it is a term used for angels in general. However, do not be confused by the same term that is used in the New Testament for born again believers. It is noteworthy that some of the versions of the Septuagint include the word "angels" in Genesis 6:2, 4. A. W. Pink suggests, "These 'sons of God,' then, appear to be angels who left their own habitation, came down to earth, and cohabited with the daughters of men."[4]

In his book *Biblical Demonology*[5], Merrill Unger presents an in-depth analysis proposing that the Genesis 6 "sons of God" are fallen angels. Both of these authors agree with the Book of Job where we receive additional insight into the identity of these "sons of God."

> *Now there was a day when the sons of God came to present themselves before the LORD, and Satan came also among them. [7]And the LORD said unto Satan, Whence comest thou? Then Satan answered the LORD, and said, From going to and fro in the earth, and from walking up and down in it.*
>
> Job 1:6-7

It is very likely that the "sons of God" that Job mentioned were angels that lived in heaven and that had not fallen with Lucifer. The fact that Lucifer knew the time that these particular angels met with the Father might indicate that at one time he had been classified as one of these "sons of God." When comparing the passages of Genesis and Job, I am inclined to agree with A.W. Pink who says that the "sons of God" mentioned in Genesis were in fact dark angels who before the rebellion had been designated as "sons of God."

The Giants

We also know from scripture that the "sons of God" or dark angels had sexual relations with women on earth (Genesis 6:2, 4). As hard as it is for us to understand, these "sons of God" took on human form and had children who became giants. These offspring were known as the Nephilim. You may ask the question, "What about the giants that were around after the flood? How were they produced?"

I would like to propose two possibilities. The first, but less likely, is that "sons of God" continued to come to earth after the flood and have relations with the women of earth. However, this scenario does not carry scriptural support. I believe that the more likely scenario is that Noah married a Cainite woman (descendant of Cain versus a descendant of Seth) who had Nephilim genes. These genes for giants would then be carried down through Noah's lineage.

First Estate

The Book of Jude supplies us with further knowledge of how some of the fallen angels came to live on earth.

> *And the angels which kept not their **first estate**, but left their own habitation, he hath reserved in everlasting chains under darkness unto the judgment of the great day.*
> *Jude 1:6*

First, I fervently believe that this verse is referring to the time of Noah. Why does Jude call them "angels" instead of using the same terminology as Genesis? The Holy Spirit inspired the New Testament writers to use the phrase "sons of God" to designate those who were born-again believers. Therefore, using the same phraseology would have created great confusion.

Second, this verse in Jude helps us understand what happened to these fallen angels after the flood. We can take for granted that all the humans killed in the flood were sent to hell. In addition, we know that the fallen angels were put "in everlasting chains." This means that they are no threat to the earth at this time, but it also lets us know that the angels who did not leave their "first estate" are still around.

If the "first estate" is the designated place where the majority of the fallen angels live, where is it located? I believe it is located somewhere in the second heaven. I tend to agree with Derek Prince that there are three heavens. In his book, *Spiritual Warfare*[6], he says, "the first heaven is the visible and natural heaven with the sun, the moon, and the stars which we see with our eyes."

The third heaven, or "heaven of heavens" (2 Chronicles 2:6), is where God dwells, and where believers go when they die. Finally, the second heaven, which is in between the other two, is where Satan and many of the fallen angels reside. Some of these fallen angels reside in the "first estate," but many illegally occupy places in the spirit realm that rightfully belong to the kingdom of heaven. When the scriptures speak of us both wrestling with and fighting these fallen angels, it is often over these illegally held seats of authority or "heavenly seats" where Jesus says we are to be seated.

*And hath raised us up together, and made us sit together in **heavenly places** in Christ Jesus:*
Ephesians 2:6

Derek Prince further states, "...all translations except the Living Bible emphasize that the headquarters of this highly-organized kingdom is in the heavenlies."[7] The Bible teaches that Satan rules from "high places" or "heavenly realms." We see this demonstrated in the Book of Daniel when an angel tells Daniel the answer to his prayer has been hindered by the Prince of Persia, a dark angel. Michael is sent to battle this Prince of Persia who is blocking the messenger en route between God's Throne in the third heaven and Daniel's location on earth. Having said this, we can establish that Satan's center of operations is in the heavenlies, not in hell. Scripture is very clear that Satan and many of the fallen angels are not yet imprisoned in hell.

*For we wrestle not against flesh and blood, but against principalities, against powers, against the rulers of the darkness of this world, against spiritual wickedness in **high places**. (NIV says **heavenly realms**)*
Ephesians 6:12

It is time that believers, especially intercessors, grasp the fact that a great number of the fallen angels dwell in the heavenlies. There are territories in the heavens that Satan and his fallen angels are permitted to occupy; I suggest these places are their "first estate."

Many lower ranking angels reside on this earth, most of which tend to inhabit people, places or objects. I will refer to the rebellious angels in the second heaven as "dark or fallen angels" and the rebellious angels on earth as "demons or evil spirits." The demons on earth are most probably spiritual in nature. However, we are living in the times that Jesus referred to, *"as the days of Noe were"* (Matthew 24:37). So we can expect to see dark angels leaving their first estate in the second heaven and coming to the earth, perhaps even mating with humans. One of the questions that I am waiting on the Lord to answer is whether there are already fallen angels who have taken on an earthly body, or is that yet to come. If we believe our Lord's prophecy, I think we better be prepared for some very extraordinary and perplexing occurrences here on earth. Some of the Hollywood film plots already depict what Jesus described when He said the last days would be like the days of Noah.

Why the Enemy is in Heavenly Places

The Lord told me on one occasion that there are several reasons that the enemy occupies many of the heavenly places. The first cause is outright sin in believers and their unwillingness to continue to repent and allow God to grow them up spiritually.

> *For when for the time ye ought to be teachers, ye have need that one teach you again which be the first principles of the oracles of God; and are become such as have need of milk, and not of strong meat. For every one that useth milk is unskillful in the word of righteousness: for he is a babe.*
> *Hebrews 5:12-13*

Ministering from Our Heavenly Seats

Second, many heavenly places are not occupied because believers have not denied themselves of the pleasures of this world.

> *And that which fell among thorns are they, which, when they have heard, go forth, and are choked with cares and riches and pleasures of this life, and bring no fruit to perfection.*
> *Luke 8:14*

Third, others have not been taken into these places because of their unwillingness to press into the strangeness of the spirit realm.

> *Jesus answered, My kingdom is not of this world: if my kingdom were of this world, then would my servants fight, that I should not be delivered to the Jews: but now is my kingdom not from hence.*
> *John 18:36*

Fourth, many believers do not comprehend the absolute necessity of a lifestyle of prayer and obedience, praying even though their prayers have no immediate effect. It is a persevering in prayer even when you do not hear from God every time.

> *Pray without ceasing.*
> *1 Thessalonians 5:17*

Fifth, they lack the passion to go after the Father through abandoned worship.

> *One thing have I desired of the LORD, that will I seek after; that I may dwell in the house of the*

> LORD *all the days of my life, to behold the beauty of the* LORD, *and to enquire in his temple.*
> *Psalm 27:4*

Demonic Powers and Spiritual Weapons

The Lord said the dark angels that are coming to the earth have enormous powers. We are about to encounter a magnitude of demonic power, which the church has not yet experienced. The Lord is releasing to His warriors unique spiritual weapons designed to fight and defeat these dark angels.

> *(For the **weapons of our warfare are not carnal**, but mighty through God to the pulling down of strong holds;)*
> *2 Corinthians 10:4*

The type of weapons Paul is talking about in this verse has nothing to do with the flesh. He is referring to weapons that are acquired in the spirit realm and utilized to fight in that realm. The list and use of the weapons in Ephesians 6 is crucial for the Christian to have and use, but the list is by no means exhaustive.

These fallen angels are dangerous beings who are coming to earth, and they have great potential to destroy people, property, and even cities. The church must pray to receive the necessary authority, weapons and power to prevent these beings from causing premature destruction all over the earth. The Lord will be providing His saints with indispensable training and equipment. The Lord is pleased to see His children stepping out in faith and fighting to take back their rightful inheritance in the heavens. Isaiah mocks these fallen angels' eventual defeat.

> *They that see thee shall narrowly look upon thee, and consider thee, saying, Is this the man that made the earth to tremble, that did shake kingdoms; ⁱ⁷That **made the world as a wilderness, and destroyed the cities thereof;** that opened not the house of his prisoners?*
>
> *Isaiah 14:16-17*

Spiritual Warfare

Throughout the body of Christ, scores of saints will receive revelations about the second heaven, the fallen angels and the final battles. Several of the things I will be sharing about the heavenlies are foundational for understanding what will transpire in the near future. God is showing intercessors many things that are absolutely amazing. One of the purposes of this book is to prepare the hearts of believers for some incredible revelatory encounters. Numerous angels of the Lord will be involved in giving these revelations and training the saints to fulfill God's purposes. During these last days, the Bible says there will be great demonically caused devastation. The Lord's angels will help and protect us. The Lord will defend His church!

> *Therefore rejoice, ye heavens, and ye that dwell in them. Woe to the inhabiters of the earth and of the sea! for the devil is come down unto you, having great wrath, because he knoweth that he hath but a short time.*
>
> *Revelation 12:12*

The supernatural powers this world will encounter must be fought in the spirit realm. The carnality that currently exists in the church will cause it to be defeated unless the church humbles herself and learns the ways of the Lord. The Lord is looking for a church that desires to know Him intimately. Those churches that step into this intimate relationship with God will flow in incredible unity and will know God's purposes for this hour. There are glorious days ahead for the church, but fierce fighting and warfare between the saints and the enemy of our souls will also characterize these times. The road ahead is difficult. The children of the Lord must "know Him" to survive the challenges coming upon us in these last days.

Today more than ever, I believe that the church will have to face many fearful sights before the rapture takes place. We do not need to debate the timing of the rapture; however, we do know that scripture says the time before the Lord's return will be like the days of Noah. There were definitely high-ranking fallen angels walking on the earth during the days of Noah.

The current atmosphere in the heavenlies is very indicative of what is about to take place. God is moving the enemy out of places where he does not belong and placing His sons in their seats of rulership. This is a process, and confrontations in the heavens take place for each seat that is reclaimed for the kingdom of God. The angelic battle in the heavens described by John the Revelator in which a third of the stars are cast down to the earth will occur not too long after we are settled in our heavenly seats.

⁴ Arthur W. Pink, *Gleanings from Genesis*, (Chicago: Moody Press 1950), pp. 93.
⁵ Merrill F. Unger, *Biblical Demonology: A Study of Spiritual Forces at Work Today*, (Grand Rapids: Kregel Publications 1994), pp. 46-52.
⁶ Derek Prince, *Spiritual Warfare*, (New Kensington: Whitaker House, 1987), pp. 20-21.
⁷ Prince, pp. 10.

7

Portals

THE NEXT few chapters discuss two primary aspects of the heavenlies, a pervasive transportation or heavenly highway system and a sophisticated communication system. The highway system is made up of what we have come to refer to as portals. Although similar to highways here on earth, these numerous portals in the spirit realm have distinctive features. They are less of a road and more like "living" tunnels suspended in space. I refer to them as living because through prayer they can be opened and closed or moved and redirected. The portals are utilized to journey from one side of the universe to the other. The portals link into the third heaven as well as to the first. Angels use these portals constantly. Saints utilize them as well via intercession. In fact, dark angels use portals to travel from hell to the earth and then into the heavens.

My challenge and yours is to not be swayed by our preconceived notions about the heavens. I used to have a very simplistic conception of the enemy and the layout of the spirit realm. Essentially, I understood that Satan and his fallen angels were primarily on earth and in hell. I believed that on occasion Satan came before the Throne of God to accuse us.

> *And I heard a loud voice saying in heaven, Now is come salvation, and strength, and the kingdom of our God, and the power of his Christ: for **the accuser of our brethren** is cast down, which accused them before our God day and night.*
> *Revelation 12:10*

My perception of the kingdom of God was also very elementary. In my limited understanding, the population of heaven was made up of God on His Throne, His angels, other heavenly beings, and a throng of resurrected believers. I did not believe the first heaven, or outer space as we call it, was inhabited. Although my description is very simplified, I think the majority of Christians have a similar understanding.

In my perception, I assumed that angels flew from place to place wherever God directed. I had never considered how this actually happens. The Lord is bringing an understanding of the truth about the spirit realm and portal travel. The angels actually voyage from heaven to earth by way of these portal systems, making use of the transportation system God created for spirit beings.

Earthly Portals

As far as believers are concerned, God is allowing us to understand how our human spirits can be transported via these portals to wherever God wants us to go in our prayers in order to accomplish His will. Initially, when God began taking me in the spirit to different places, angels would come and literally carry me in the spirit to these places. As these trips became more frequent, God began opening my eyes to see the portals that this book describes. God may take your spirit via these portals to another country. Once I was taken to Pakistan to agree with another intercessor for what God wanted to accomplish there. I saw this believer in a room kneeling in prayer.

On one of my earliest trips, angels came and took me to a house where they allowed me to watch as they fought with the demons that inhabited the house. The angels went through the house and cleaned out all of the demons. They fought and wrestled with these demons while I just observed and interceded. When they were done, the angels carried my spirit back to our church. On another occasion, the angels came and took me to a street where a man lay dying on the sidewalk from a chest wound and the Lord had me pray for him. Then the angels returned me to the church.

Portal Encounter

I am not alone in these experiences. Many intercessors tell similar stories. I have included an excerpt of an experience that was recently shared with me by a young married couple in our congregation. This episode demonstrates another unexpected aspect of portal travel during intercession. There can be agreement and interaction between saints while in the spirit realm.

Ministering from Our Heavenly Seats

We were lying in bed talking about the conference that was currently going on at our church. Then we began worshipping and singing in the spirit as a very strong, sweet presence of the Lord came over our room. Mrs. M saw a vision of a circle of vibrating light that was just over her as she lay in the bed. As she looked at the center of the bright light that was centered over her, circles of light would ripple out to the edge. Then the light moved and centered over Mr. M.

Just as that happened, we both experienced the same thing. A doorway or gate came from above down over us, through us and around us. We actually went through a gateway – but it went around us rather than us going through it. We both asked each other at the same time "Did you feel that?" and tried to explain it. Mr. M. was reminded of a scripture the Lord had been showing him that day and wanted to declare it over us so he read out loud all of 2 Peter 1. Here are the most important verses:

> *For so an entrance shall be ministered unto you abundantly into the everlasting kingdom of our Lord and Saviour Jesus Christ. ...We have also a more sure word of prophecy; whereunto ye do well that ye take heed, as unto a light that shineth in a dark place, until the day dawn, and the day star arise in your hearts:*
>
> *2 Peter 1:11, 19*

After he read the passage, we continued to worship and could tell that we were in the spirit although we were still able to talk to each other. Then we began to sense that our spirits were somewhere other than our bedroom. We could each hear the dialogue of people in a room and could even see things.

Portals

Mrs. M. clearly saw that we were in a room that was lit by a candle. A group of people were gathered to perform a ritualistic ceremony. Mr. M. spoke the words "put down the list" and Mrs. M. immediately saw a list lying on a small table in the center of the room next to the candle. It was a hand written list, and she could see the names of people in our church and even the people attending the conference.

We agreed at this point that we were witnessing a meeting that was happening at the B&B community center. This is a place solely dedicated to the worship of the enemy, where many of his people gather. This is a central place we have found during our research on finding the high places in Dallas.

Mr. M. said the name "Cindy" and repeated the words "put down the list," and we could tell that confusion and tension had entered the room, several people began arguing with each other. A man turned, saw Mr. M. and asked, "What right do you have to be here?"

Mrs. M. felt like she was close to the girl named Cindy and began talking to her and telling her not to be afraid and that Jesus loved her. Cindy was very afraid and didn't know what to do.

Dialogue was going on that we could hear and we continued to talk to each other and explain the things that we were seeing. We were there but at the same time we were still in our bed able to talk to each other.

Then we began pleading the blood over Cindy and then over the room. We kept saying, "fill the room with the blood of Jesus, fill the room with the blood" over and over. There was complete chaos in the room at this point.

Ministering from Our Heavenly Seats

Suddenly Mr. M. felt like he had been pushed outside of the room and the building and was standing 10 feet or so in front of the doorway. Mrs. M. was still in the room pleading the blood.

Mr. M saw and began confronting a demonic being that was standing in front of the doorway. He had the body of a man and was very large, but he had the head of a ram with huge round circular horns. His face and body had a reddish hue as if his blood was boiling underneath. Mr. M. was describing what he saw and immediately Mrs. M. saw the being as well and was now out in front of the building with him. Mr. M ran up to the being and brought his arms down with clenched fists over the being's head and struck him between the eyes. At this point Mr. M. was pulled out of the spirit completely and was back in our room. Mrs. M. was still there but was more aware of our room at this point... [The couple goes on to explain other experiences after this incident.]

Mr. & Mrs. S.M., February 8, 2002

These dear ones while praying together on earth in agreement for God's purposes brought confusion into the camp of the kingdom of darkness and reached out with the precious blood of Jesus to those who were captive.

> *Verily I say unto you, Whatsoever ye shall bind on earth shall be bound in heaven: and whatsoever ye shall loose on earth shall be loosed in heaven. Again I say unto you, That if two of you shall agree on earth as touching any thing that they shall ask, it shall be done for them*

> *of my Father which is in heaven. For where two or three are gathered together in my name, there am I in the midst of them.*
> *Matthew 18:18-20*

Portals to Hell

As I mentioned in my book *Ministering with Angels*, my original portal travels were on earth. Later they shifted to hell and then into the second and third heavens.

You may question the scriptural basis for believers visiting hell. King David spoke of his spirit being taken to heaven, to hell and in the seas.

> *If I ascend up into heaven, thou art there: if I make my bed in hell, behold, thou art there. If I take the wings of the morning, and dwell in the uttermost parts of the sea; Even there shall thy hand lead me, and thy right hand shall hold me.*
> *Psalm 139:8-10*

After these initial trips across the earth, there was a short season where the Lord took me into the corridors of hell. My first encounters in hell were with figures in dark hooded robes walking freely about. They had their heads bowed, but as I walked up to them they lifted their heads to acknowledge me. Their faces looked like living skeletons. Their horrendous appearance and the spirit of fear that attacked me caused me to cry out to the Lord, and immediately He pulled me out of hell. At first these trips created a great deal of fear in me as I was still a novice in the spirit realm.

Ministering from Our Heavenly Seats

Some of the corridors of hell were lined with cells where beings were imprisoned and could not freely move around in hell itself. The beings in this cellblock area were full of hopelessness, despair, torment and emanated feelings of ultimate abandonment. This encounter brought me to understand the horrible reality of hell in a way that sermons and scriptures were not able to capture. When I experienced hell myself, the terror of being forever separated from God became a reality to me. Now when I share Christ with the lost, I have a passion for their salvation that I did not have before. I know what they are facing if they do not turn to Jesus Christ as their personal Savior.

Once when the Lord led me through a passageway in hell, I saw a tall, dignified dark spirit with a black cape and helmet. He was sitting on what appeared to be a throne. When he saw me coming toward him, he walked over to a portal and suddenly disappeared. Several months later, the Lord took me to an area in the second heaven controlled by the enemy. There I encountered this same dark angel again. The Lord said that he was a high-ranking assassin spirit, and he definitely looked the part. Later I also ran across the hooded skeletons in the second heaven. These trips to hell taught me that dark angels could travel from locations here on earth to hell and back out into the heavenlies.

These sights and scenes and the demonic beings themselves evoked a lot of fear. After several such encounters, the Lord began to teach me not to fear. God had me in His hand, and like Job, nothing could harm me without His permission. I might not always sense the presence of the Lord or His angels, but He is still there. He promises, *"I will never leave thee nor forsake thee"* (Hebrews 13:5) and *"Yea, though I walk through the valley of the shadow of death I will fear no evil for thou art with me"* (Psalm 23:4).

Although our experiences may even be in hell and we might appear to fail in our assignment, the Lord is always there to rescue, strengthen and encourage us. God did not view this experience as a failure but as a lesson. When faced with an extremely difficult situation like this, always remember that you can cry out to the Lord. He is forever there, right beside you. Through this experience, the Lord put a determination in my heart to stand fast and not run when confronted by the enemy.

> *Notwithstanding the Lord stood with me, and strengthened me; ... And the Lord shall deliver me from every evil work, and will preserve me unto his heavenly kingdom: to whom be glory for ever and ever. Amen.*
> 2 Timothy 4:17a-18

If you obey the Lord and trust Him, you will continue to grow and step into higher levels of the Spirit. We must purpose to have greater faith to endure hardship and overcome fear. The Lord teaches us to more fully trust His perfect love.

> *There is no fear in love; but perfect love casteth out fear: because fear hath torment. He that feareth is not made perfect in love.*
> 1 John 4:18

Portals of the Second Heaven

The next season of portal travel came as the Lord began taking me into the second heaven. The portals in the second heaven are uniquely different from the ones that spread out across the earth. My pilgrimage into the second heaven took many months in prayer. Part of the process for me involved going through various gates and doorways that were guarded by one or more dark angels. The way that I gained access was different for almost every gate. God usually assigned one or more angels to accompany and help me.

Warfare normally occurred at each entry point, and the Lord or His angels would give me weapons to use in fighting or wrestling with the different dark angels. At times I was instructed to speak certain words that would have devastating results on the enemy.

The appearance of the dark angels varied. Most of them appeared alien-like. Creatures in science fiction movies often look similar to the demonic beings in the spirit realm. There are also beings that have a human-like appearance. For example, I once came upon an ugly, bald man with short horns all over his head. This was a terribly wicked creature.

Though you gain victories after battling at the gates, once inside there are frequently additional confrontations; however, most of the contesting is at the gates. During one encounter I was not able to enter a gate because I did not have sufficient authority nor did the angels who were with me. I needed a higher-ranking angel of the Lord to go with me. The Lord sent the necessary angel, and I continued my journey. You could relate this to needing a certain level of security clearance in the natural.

These incredible journeys through the second heaven took place quite often. On many occasions, there were daily excursions into the heavens. Although it seemed like I was fighting alone, I know that God had others coming into agreement with me in prayer during these battles. Many times these intercessors did not realize what their intercession was accomplishing. Whenever God would allow me to share my experiences with them, I would.

At some of the doorways and gates, the Lord would have me take things away from the enemy. Often I had no clue as to what I had taken from them; I would have to do this by faith. These encounters with dark angels can feel very physical in nature. I have been cursed, threatened, and I have felt as if I was being choked and stabbed. At times God had me fight and resist, and there were other times I was told to just stand still. Most of the time I spoke in tongues when dealing with the dark angels; on occasion, God would give me the interpretation.

The great thing about warring in the spirit realm is that when God sends you to "take the land," you **will** be victorious. I have never lost a battle in the heavens; however, due to the lack of corporate intercession, I have had my assignment postponed. When God wants something accomplished – it gets done.

Each victory brought additional authority, and I would receive new swords, weapons, or additional markings on my spiritual vestments. What is the benefit of greater authority? The demonic world takes note of the markings on your spirit man. They must yield to authority. If you have achieved a certain level of authority, when you speak, the enemy has to obey. Remember it was demonic spirits who acknowledged both Jesus and Paul's spiritual authority to command them but refused to obey the sons of Sceva who perhaps used the same words trying to exert spiritual authority that they did not possess. In fact, the sons of Sceva discovered how powerful and dangerous demonic spirits are.

Ministering from Our Heavenly Seats

> *Then certain of the vagabond Jews, exorcists, took upon them to call over them which had evil spirits the name of the Lord Jesus, saying, We adjure you by Jesus whom Paul preacheth. And there were seven sons of one Sceva, a Jew, and chief of the priests, which did so. And the evil spirit answered and said, Jesus I know, and Paul I know; but who are ye? And the man in whom the evil spirit was leaped on them, and overcame them, and prevailed against them, so that they fled out of that house naked and wounded.*
> *Acts 19:13-16*

If Christ is dwelling in you, then essentially the word of the Lord is speaking through you. The enemy is intimidated when he sees Christ in us rather than seeing us.

Creating an Open Heaven

Through intercession, we are literally clearing out the portals that were inhabited by the enemy but which now bring us an open heaven over our church. The intercessors that came after me did not face as many hindrances. They quickly passed through areas that had already been secured for the kingdom of God. As God sends new families to our church, it is interesting to note how He usually anoints at least one individual in the family for intercession. These new intercessors were quickly launched into places in the spirit realm that took us months or even years to attain. It is like the story Jesus told of the wages being the same for all the workers in the harvest field even though some had put in more hours than others (Matthew 20:1-16).

Portals

Stepping out into the wonders of the kingdom of God and the spirit realm can be very disconcerting. Adequately conveying to others what the Lord has revealed to you during intercession is a tricky proposition.

> *But as it is written, Eye hath not seen, nor ear heard, neither have entered into the heart of man, the things which God hath prepared for them that love him. But God hath revealed them unto us by his Spirit: for the Spirit searcheth all things, yea, the deep things of God.*
> *1 Corinthians 2:9-10*

You might not have ever thought it possible you could be the one to see or hear these marvelous revelations. However, God continually reveals the deeper mysteries of His kingdom to those who are communing with Him.

I have been just a small part of the immense anointing that God has prepared for His people. I have been blessed to have a senior pastor who flows in a powerful, revelatory gifting. Our intercessors constantly receive powerful revelations and visions of the wonders of the kingdom of God. However, the good news is that we are beginning to hear confirming reports coming in from around the globe about the great revelations God is giving to His saints.

The toughest thing for saints in the coming years will be enduring harsh attacks from other believers within the church. An angry religious spirit will rise up in many and speak evil against those who report having heavenly experiences. Do not be swayed by the negative words that will be spoken against you. Stand strong.

> *Blessed are ye, when men shall hate you, and when they shall separate you from their company, and shall reproach you, and cast out your name as evil, for the Son of man's sake. Rejoice ye in that day, and leap for joy: for, behold, your reward is great in heaven: for in the like manner did their fathers unto the prophets.*
> *Luke 6:22-23*

Many believers will be invited by the Lord to do amazing things in the spirit realm, but this will not come without a price. I would hope that you could avoid the criticisms and evil words that always come to those who follow the Lord's commands. Moreover, I want to reassure intercessors that these experiences are of the Lord and to be prepared for attacks of fear when these experiences begin.

> *For, when we were come into Macedonia, our flesh had no rest,* ***but we were troubled on every side; without were fightings, within were fears****.*
> *2 Corinthians 7:5*

During these experiences, the enemy would either try to convince me I was going insane or he wanted me to think they were demonically induced. He was willing to do anything to stop my quest.

I estimate that 95% of all my experiences in the spirit realm have come during intercession at church, and because of the nature of spiritual warfare other intercessors were involved. Even though they may not have realized they were assisting me in the spirit, the other intercessors played a significant role in God's purposes. The New Testament teaches a pattern of corporate intercession.

> *Again I say unto you, That if two of you shall agree on earth as touching any thing that they shall ask, it shall be done for them of my Father which is in heaven.*
> *Matthew 18:19*

Generally, the Lord does not have us operate alone in the spirit realm. Remember that in the Garden of Gethsemane Jesus wanted others nearby praying with Him even though they did not realize the significance of what was happening.

Maturing in our Heavenly Walk

As the Lord began taking my spirit through various portals in the second heaven, I began to realize the immensity of the heavens. As you mature in the Lord through your journeys into the heavenlies, the Lord will ask you to take some steps of faith that He did not require of you in the earlier stages. For instance, I once came to a place where there were at least fifty portal openings, and after receiving instructions from the Lord I was able by faith to make myself take the precise entrance. This parallels directly with our walk in the Lord here on earth, where the Holy Spirit guides us in the direction we must go, but He does not force us to take His path. Created with free wills, we must come into agreement and obediently cooperate with the Holy Spirit. There are instances when we do not want to follow the prompting of the Holy Spirit. Unfortunately, if we do not conform to the Spirit's leading, we succumb to disobedience.

God is asking His children to step into a higher dimension. When the Psalmist says, *"Thy word is a light unto my path,"* (Psalm 119:105) it infers that we do not know the way, and that we have not walked this way before. The more unfamiliar the path, as are these visits to the second heaven, the more closely you must listen to and obey the voice of God. God **never** deviates from His written Word, but He sure makes you listen and follow Him closely. When you enter the spirit realm, you do whatever God directs and go wherever He sends you. In the heavenlies, the Word of God is still our foundation; and exactly as He does here on earth, the Holy Spirit leads and guides us.

> *Trust in the LORD with all thine heart; and lean not unto thine own understanding. In all thy ways acknowledge him, and he shall direct thy paths.*
> *Proverbs 3:5-6*

I have been taught almost as much in the spirit realm as I have been here on earth. As curious as it sounds, the portals can be pathways to knowledge, wisdom and understanding. As the Lord takes you to various places in the spirit, you will be constantly learning God's ways. Often you will find yourself involved in conversations with either the Lord or His angels. These conversations may be entirely in tongues; nevertheless, God is teaching and strengthening your spirit even when you do not grasp everything with your mind.

> *And I will bring the blind by a way that they knew not; I will lead them in paths that they have not known: I will make darkness light before them, and crooked things straight. These things will I do unto them, and not forsake them.*
> *Isaiah 42:16*

Physical Translations

Many are going to move from seeing things in the heavenlies, such as portals, to using them. This is a big jump! The portals that exist, as well as the many that God is going to open up, will be used by intercessors to go places to be in agreement with God's purposes. In the future, many portals will become active passageways for saints to travel on the Father's business. I am talking about physical translations. Many saints will be translated regularly around the globe. I am certain the Holy Spirit will strictly regulate and guard these portals. Many churches will have permanent portal openings located somewhere within their facilities.

Vision of the Portal to Dallas

Recently, I received the following open vision from Pastor Robert Fulton of Clouds of Glory Church in Brooklyn, New York. Pastor Fulton did not know that I was writing this book and that an entire chapter was dedicated to the topic of portals. Even though the book was almost completed, the Lord has led me to include a summary of this vision with the permission of Pastor Fulton.

While in worship with our small congregation, my attention was drawn to the back wall. As I was drawn to the wall, a portal opened. I went through the portal and ended up in the balcony of Lakewood Church in Dallas, Texas. Pastor Crawford saw me come through the portal and said to the congregation, "Hey, there's Robert." I walked down from the balcony to the main floor where he was, and we talked.

Ministering from Our Heavenly Seats

The next day I caught a flight from Dallas to New York. I tried to explain to my manager the reason for my lateness to work. In doing so I convinced him to attend our church the upcoming Sunday to see for himself whether the things I was saying to him were true. The following Sunday as he was with us in worship, I felt the unction of the Lord to invite him to go with me through the portal. As we were going into the portal, I began witnessing to him. He was in somewhat of a state of shock. I just continued to witness to him about the love of Jesus Christ and assured him that what he was experiencing was scriptural. We went through the portal and Pastor Crawford again said to the congregation, "Hey, here's Robert again." We went downstairs from the balcony to the main floor, and I continued ministering Jesus to him. At Lakewood, my manager accepted Jesus as his Lord and Savior. I don't know if we went back to New York through the portal or caught a plane.

When my manager went back to work, he was witnessing about his newfound salvation in Jesus and how Jesus is real. With much zeal and emotion he was saying that what had happened to Robert last week happened to me, too. He made such a stir and was so excited that many from the job came to the church. From that point on, the church rapidly began to grow. People heard about the portal between Lakewood and my church. We had to use the room behind where we now worship as an overflow room, and we had to go to two morning services. Also our intercessors' group grew large.

As to the portal, there was no time or space associated with going through the portal. It seemed as if once you walked in, you walked out on the other side. There was nothing to associate how long, in terms of time, it took to travel from New York to Dallas, nor was there any recollection in terms of space as to how long the portal was.

Portals

Many people came and accepted Jesus Christ, some of them even experienced walking through the portal. We were now able to go back and forth from New York to Dallas and Dallas to New York without catching a flight. As word of this got out, a family that at one time was a part of our congregation came. I had to treat them with a sharp hand. Some people were coming just to experience what God was doing in regard to the portal. I went through the portal, and Pastor Paul came back through the portal to Cloud of Glory Tabernacle with me.

The Lord instructed me to bring the children of the family through the portal, and Pastor Paul would bring the husband and wife through. Prior to us proceeding through the portal, I could see that the husband was skeptical while the wife was more anxious. I began ministering the Word of God to them of how this is scriptural in that the Spirit of the Lord would take Elijah from place to place, 1 Kings 18:7-12. The Spirit of Lord also did this in the life of Philip the Evangelist after the angel told him to join the Ethiopian eunuch, Acts 8:26-40. I also spoke to the children. The eldest son was 15 years old at this time and in a rebellious state. I told him that he could either repent now or just sit while the rest of his family shared the portal experience. I paid particular attention to the younger son who was filled with excitement and ready to experience a new move of the Lord. This younger son had experienced seeing angels in our church before. He loves the Lord and whatever the Lord is doing.

I proceeded by taking the children through the portal, and the next thing we knew we were in Lakewood. Pastor Paul took the parents through the portal. The Lord had stationed two angels on both sides of the portal. Some in our congregation were able to see these angels.

Ministering from Our Heavenly Seats

After that, another brother I know who lives in the Bronx came to the church with his wife. He left his home church and pastor with the sole intent of wanting to experience going through the portal. I shared with him that we just do not go through the portal at our will, only by direction from the Lord. The Lord did not allow him to go through the portal; however, the Lord was gracious to his wife by allowing her to go through.

As the fame of what God was doing spread, we felt we needed to have some sort of safeguard so that people would not get too close and accidentally fall through the portal. We placed a barrier around the portal of four silver poles with a red rope between them just as you see in a bank.

One person came into the church and just ran into the portal. He ran in and out of the portal just to experience it because he had never experienced it before. However, when he came back out, ten years had been instantaneously added to his life. The aging was more internal than external except that his hair turned completely white. He didn't notice any change so we handed him a mirror so that he could see the results of his sin. After that he repented to the Lord, and we prayed and laid hands on him. The Lord restored his health back to what it was and changed his hair color back to its normal color except for his sideburns and beard, which remained white as a reminder that this would happen to those who would be rebellious.

We were not to go through the portal just at random but only as the Lord would guide us. The Lord let us know that the reason only ten years was added to his life was because he did not stay. He went in the portal and came right out. Had he stayed longer, ninety years would have been added to his life, and he would have died. After this, the Lord gave my immediate family and our lead intercessor the release to go through the portal at will. He allowed us to bring one guest with us anytime we went through the portal. I believe the Lord gave us this liberty because we recognized our responsibility. We would not just go through the portal to Lakewood at our leisure; we would wait for the leading of the Lord. There were times when the members of Lakewood would come through the portal to Cloud of Glory Tabernacle.

The vision ceased at this point as I began to pray saying to the Lord that I appreciated what He is showing to me, and more than anything I want more of Him. Then the vision resumed.

The intercessors were praying with more intensity as I was about to minister the Word concerning the life of Elijah. I began to feel a pull towards the portal; the Lord was pulling us to go through the portal to Lakewood. Our entire congregation went through the portal to Lakewood.

While all this was going on, the Dallas Fire Department came to Lakewood because the church had caught on fire. The neighbors came out to watch as the church was on fire but not being consumed. The fire continued on for three days. However, we did not realize three days had passed because we were caught away in the Spirit. The neighboring communities came to see this magnificent sight. A church on fire but not consumed. No one from the outside could get into the church building.

All of a sudden I saw a New York City fireman fall through the portal in the balcony that linked Cloud of Glory Tabernacle to Lakewood Church. I ran to the balcony and grabbed him. He had aged considerably. I took him back through the portal to New York. The same thing was happening

Ministering from Our Heavenly Seats

to our building, it was on fire but not being consumed. So I helped the fireman outside the building. He fell to the ground. He was near death. He was very old. I took his hat off. His hair was all white.

I prayed for him, and right there he received the Lord Jesus Christ, and God restored him back to health. The firemen were looking at their comrade and the building on fire but not being consumed. I asked the firemen if they believed in the Lord Jesus Christ and if any of them wanted to be saved. The firemen raised their hands and received Jesus that night. The Lord also stationed two angels at the front door of the building with their swords drawn. A third angel came for me and the fireman who fell through the portal to bring us into the building and back through the portal to Lakewood. Before we went in, I instructed the firemen to set a boundary around the main entrance of the building so that no one would venture inside the building.

Many people came to see what was happening. I instructed the firemen to tell people that this has nothing to do with Mary. I told them that there were to be no Hail Mary's but Hail Jesus. I asked them to repeat "No Hail Mary but Hail Jesus. Jesus is King of Kings. Jesus is Lord of Lords." I told them to tell the people this is not about Mary, it is about Jesus. There is no other name under heaven given among men by which we must be saved. They were repeating that. I also told them to repeat, "We believe that Jesus Christ died on the cross; we believe that Jesus was in the grave three days and three nights. He rose on the third day, and that He is sitting on the right hand of the power of God."

The vision ended.

 Counterfeit of Satan

GOD CREATED man to have a personal relationship with Him. Satan realizes that when hungry hearts fail to find the Lord, they often turn to the occult or other world religions.

We know that Satan counterfeits most, if not all, of the things of the Lord. For example, scripture mentions that there are false Christs, false prophets, false teachers and false apostles. Spiritual offices exist within the kingdom of darkness, and individuals who operate in these offices flow in false gifts and anointings that are counterfeits or perversions of the gifts and anointings that operate in the kingdom of God.

> *For there shall arise false Christs, and false prophets, and shall shew great signs and wonders; insomuch that, if it were possible, they shall deceive the very elect. Behold, I have told you before. Wherefore if they shall say unto you,*

> *Behold, he is in the desert; go not forth: behold,*
> *he is in the secret chambers; believe it not.*
> *Matthew 24:24-26*

In Acts 16, we see the counterfeit of the gift of prophecy being used; Paul called it the spirit of divination. The same counterfeiting goes on today. Satan is utilizing God's creation for his own purposes, both in the natural and in the spirit realm.

In this chapter, I want to carefully describe the counterfeit use of spiritual portals and transportation systems, so we can better understand the deceptions of our enemy. I need to make it very clear that when I speak of being taken in the spirit, I am **not** talking about astral projection or astral traveling. Astral projection is the enemy's counterfeit of God taking a person's spirit someplace while their physical body stays where it is in intercession.

> *But evil men and seducers shall wax worse and*
> *worse, deceiving, and being deceived.*
> *2 Timothy 3:13*

Astral Travel vs. God Taking Us in the Spirit

There is an enormous difference between astral travel and God taking us somewhere by His Holy Spirit. When you are involved in astral travel, Satan, the enemy of our souls, is the one taking your spirit. James says when sin is finished it brings forth death, and in the case of astral travel, your very life is in the hands of Satan.

When an unbeliever is astral traveling, his spirit is still connected by what Solomon called the "silver cord."

*Or ever the **silver cord** be loosed, or the golden bowl be broken, or the pitcher be broken at the fountain, or the wheel broken at the cistern. Then shall the dust return to the earth as it was: and the spirit shall return unto God who gave it.*
Ecclesiastes 12:6-7

If you read secular books on astral projecting, you will find that those who astral travel know about the silver cord. They realize it is their lifeline, but still the majority of them have no idea of the imminent dangers in astral projecting. What are the dangers? The primary danger involves the silver cord or the connection that extends between a person's stationary body and the traveling spirit. The person will die immediately if this cord is severed. Another serious danger is deception. Astral projectionists are manipulated and deceived by Satan into believing many lies. Remember Satan is the father of lies and his most believable ones include a generous amount of truth that is intertwined with deception.

One particular book encouraged people to try astral projection because it was better and easier than traveling the world in the natural. The author said it was cheaper, more exhilarating and you never have to leave home. It is tragic how many people gamble with their lives, experimenting in the supernatural realm in this way. You need to understand, that these people think they can journey into the past and trek into the future. Whether we like it or not, man is bound by time.

Ministering from Our Heavenly Seats

> *A time to be born, and a time to die; ... so that no man can find out the work that God maketh from the beginning to the end.*
> *Ecclesiastes 3:2a, 11b*

However, Satan can deceive people into believing they can travel through time. Some report they see relatives that have been dead for many years or what their own life will be like in the future. As strange as all this sounds, it is very real and exciting to these astral travelers. Satan has the ability to create truly a "virtual" reality that appears so real it is almost impossible to detect the deception without the help of the Lord.

Another important distinction between astral traveling and the Lord taking you somewhere in the spirit has to do with who initiates it. In the book, *Astral Travel for Beginners*, Richard Webster markets astral travel as the ability to travel free whenever and wherever you want. He described it as very useful, recommending astral travel as a way to find out what people think about you. He also suggests it as a cheap alternative to world travel or checking-in on family and friends. Finally he claims that, "You can travel backwards and forwards through time. **Once you can astral travel whenever you wish**, you will never suffer from boredom again"[8] (emphasis mine).

When the Lord takes you somewhere in the spirit, He initiates it. The majority of the time, the Lord does not tell you where He is taking you. It is critical that you understand that **we cannot initiate a trip into the spirit realm**. We do not enter our prayer time and tell the Lord to take us to China because we want to intercede for their churches. God will initiate and empower whatever He wants us to do, not what we want to do.

Activities of Astral Projectionists

Once the Lord told me in the middle of the week that there would be some astral projectionists in the service on the following Sunday. The next Sunday night, as I was praying before the service started, the Lord took me through an earthly portal into someone's home. It was the home of one of the individuals who was projecting into the service. He was lying on the floor, unclothed and badly bruised. He appeared dead, but the Lord said he was not. (If you do any research on this activity, you will find that astral projectionists prefer to project while in the nude.) There were at least two astral projectionists in the service that night, which were seen by other members of our church. One of our watchmen actually saw the silver cord for one of the astral projectionists. There is no reason to curse them or become angry. In fact, we prayed for their salvation. They are pawns of Satan and need the love of the Lord.

I have had to deal with astral projectionists interrupting my sleep trying to frighten me. Several members in our church have also had similar experiences. These astral projectionists can invade your dreams and cause you to experience some strange things. I have been startled in the middle of the night with a human spirit floating right in front of me. It was a very scary ordeal. I began to pray and asked the Lord, "What is going on?" I had been very diligent to plead the blood of Jesus over my family and home every night and to break off all assignments and curses that the enemy may have released against us. However, the Lord said that I also needed to break off attacks of human spirits. When I started this practice, the attacks from human spirits ceased.

Ministering from Our Heavenly Seats

If you are walking daily with the Lord and submitting to His training program for your spiritual development, there will be occasions when the training seems very strange. Like with Job, God may allow the enemy a certain amount of freedom in order to bring us to an even deeper understanding of His ways and a greater inheritance in Him. There have been times when the Lord has shown me these realms where the enemy takes many astral projectionists to deceive them. These travelers learn things about the spirit realm and how it works, but because the enemy is guiding and teaching them, it is a perverted experience.

I have shared at length this information regarding astral projection because it is essential to understanding the spirit realm in a greater measure. Why is an understanding so essential? First, astral projection is the counterfeit of what God is currently revealing to the body of Christ in these last days. Second, some of the critics of this book will accuse us of being astral travelers, which we are definitely not. I am thankful that the Lord is showing us the enemy's strategy and how to deal with his devices.

> *Lest Satan should get an advantage of us: for we are not ignorant of his devices.*
> *2 Corinthians 2:11*

---

[8] Richard Webster, *Astral Projecting for Beginners*, (St. Paul: Llewellyn Publications, 1998), pp. XX.

9 Communications in the Heavenlies

THE COMMUNICATION network in the heavenlies is extraordinary. Information is sent and received in the blink of an eye. Scripture tells us that every word we speak is being recorded in heaven, and that includes every prayer that has ever been or ever will be voiced.

> *But I say unto you, That every idle word that men shall speak, they shall give account thereof in the day of judgment.*
> *Matthew 12:36*

The Lord's mind is vast and the communication system in heaven, which extends into the second heaven, is one of the manifestations of the incredible mind of God. God is calling His church to interact with His extraordinary communication system. Scripture tells us about the mind of Christ and speaks of how vast and infinite it really is. During times of intercession, the Lord may ask you to minister in one of these critical areas of communication. As you do, you will come to appreciate the vastness of the Lord's mind.

> *For who hath known the mind of the Lord, that he may instruct him? But we have the mind of Christ.*
>
> *1 Corinthians 2:16*

Angels have Purpose

Before the Lord shared this revelation about the communication systems with me, I simply thought that everything you ever said or did was stored in God's mind or being. I never realized that there was a spiritual "hardware system" in place and that angels were responsible for its operation. We know the scriptures that tell us about the record books that are kept. Revelation 20:12 says, the books will be opened and everyone will be judged based on what is written in them.

> *And I saw the dead, small and great, stand before God; and the books were opened: and another book was opened, which is the book of life: and the dead were judged out of those things which were written in the books, according to their works.*
>
> *Revelation 20:12*

Communications in the Heavenlies

Angels were created to perform a variety of functions in the spirit realm besides giving praises to God, warring with the enemy and guarding believers. The angels who work in the communications areas are highly skilled in the technical aspects of their jobs.

According to the Book of Revelation, God is going to use the angels in unprecedented ways in these last days. They are being sent to minister and partner with the saints. The Father is sending forth His angels even now to give us information about the places to which we are being sent to minister. They also come to reveal the strategy the enemy will use to try to defeat us. No matter how God chooses to utilize His angels, we must remember that the Holy Spirit is ultimately the One who tells us what to expect and what our strategy should be. God often uses the angels as messengers to pass on the information. We see an example of this in Acts with Cornelius.

> *He saw in a vision evidently about the ninth hour of the day an angel of God coming in to him, and saying unto him, Cornelius. And when he looked on him, he was afraid, and said, What is it, Lord? And he said unto him, Thy prayers and thine alms are come up for a memorial before God.*
> *Acts 10:3-4*

Communication Centers in the Heavenlies

There is an enormous communication center in the heaven of heavens. This area is the nerve center for a great amount of angelic activity and intercessory work. Many times the Lord has had me "minister" or work in this center in the third heaven, and I have witnessed other intercessors ministering in this area as well. A throng of angels and numerous saints operate this extraordinary system that extends throughout the heavenlies.

I am amazed at the speed in which everything is carried out. The various languages spoken in these communication areas are spoken at a rapid pace and include a unique numeric language. There are angels that coordinate the activities of the various angelic groups, as well as the messages that are sent. One of many operations in this center is to track prayers that are coming in and answers to prayers that are going back to the earth. Many of the messages sent from heaven represent answered prayers; others represent revelations and prophetic words. In addition, there is a tremendous amount of information stored. All the activity that goes on in heaven, in the heavenlies, in hell and on earth is meticulously tracked by the information gathering systems God has created.

The Bible speaks to this information gathering in several passages including,

> **INFORMATION ABOUT YOUR BODY:** *Are not five sparrows sold for two farthings, and not one of them is forgotten before God?* ***But even the very hairs of your head are all numbered.*** *Fear not therefore: ye are of more value than many sparrows.*
> *Luke 12:6-7*

Communications in the Heavenlies

INFORMATION ABOUT YOUR SOUL:
*Likewise, I say unto you, there is joy in the presence of the angels of God **over one sinner that repenteth**.*
Luke 15:10

INFORMATION ABOUT YOUR SINS:
*For if the word spoken by angels was stedfast, **and every transgression and disobedience** received a just recompence of reward;*
Hebrews 2:2

INFORMATION ABOUT YOUR LIFE:
*A fiery stream issued and came forth from before him: thousand thousands ministered unto him, and ten thousand times ten thousand stood before him: the judgment was set, **and the books were opened**.*
Daniel 7:10

*And I saw the dead, small and great, stand before God; **and the books were opened:** and another book was opened, which is the book of life: and the dead were judged out of those things which were written in the books, according to their works.*
Revelation 20:12

The communication center is an area that is bustling with activity, and angels are dispatched continuously. Many of their assignments are distributed from here. Once again, everything is being documented. Satan is well informed about this sphere of operations in heaven.

Besides the main communication center in heaven, there is also a network of smaller communication stations scattered throughout the heavenlies. The Lord's angels operate many of these communication stations with the assistance of the saints. Unfortunately, the enemy forces of the dark realm have gained control of some of these stations in the second heaven due to the lack of believers stepping into their places of authority. The enemy does not have to battle for many of the positions he holds in the heavenlies because the believers God purposed to occupy these positions are not there.

Saints Taking their Seats

It is vital that the saints wake up and press into the Lord to find out what place and position they are called to occupy. As the saints come into the revelation that the Lord requires in order to minister from their "heavenly seats," we will see a significant change in the spiritual dynamics of this earth. For hundreds of years the enemy has kept the church in the dark concerning the deeper places that can be found in God. The Lord is literally taking the lid off and showing His children their inheritance. In the battles against the enemy in these last days, the Lord's church will need to occupy their heavenly places in order to be victorious.

Communications Fueled by Intercession

Every healthy functional church should be a communication center for the Lord. The basic requirement is intercession. If a church does not intercede, then it cannot take advantage of the additional information God is making available to the church and its leaders. In addition, every healthy church should have regular interactions with the angelic. There should be regular visitations of angels with the senior pastor, as well as other leaders and the general congregation. The church that partners with the angelic will most likely be given the gift of divers tongues. It is imperative to flow in divers tongues to effectively communicate with the angels.

The other essential element for a church to be an effective communication center is to have everyone flowing under the established authority structure. Angels will not interact with a church whose leaders are not obedient and submitted to the Lord and His purposes. Respect for and proper administration of authority is absolutely essential before angelic or heavenly ministry can be conducted. I would highly recommend two excellent books about authority, *Under Cover* by John Bevere[9] and *Authority and Submission* by Watchman Nee[10].

This aspect of a church being a communication center is crucial. God has relied on intercessors throughout the history of mankind, and He has changed history through the efforts of intercessors like Moses and Nehemiah.

> *And I sought for a man among them, that should make up the hedge, and stand in the gap before me for the land, that I should not destroy it: but I found none.*
>
> *Ezekiel 22:30*

However, in these last days He is calling forth His church to come into a higher dimension of intercession, intercession at a corporate level. He is gifting pastors and churches with unique corporate intercessory anointings. These anointings are unlike anything the church has ever seen before and will bring incredible unity to a local body. However, the requirement will be a complete overhaul and a rebirth of the prayer ministry. You cannot hold on to past methods and flow in this new dimension of intercession.

Divers Tongues

In *Ministering with Angels*, I introduced the significance of the recent revelation of the gift of divers tongues. You should earnestly seek the Lord for this gift! Most people tend to be in the midst of prayer when the Lord takes them some place in the spirit. We have found that praying in divers tongues enables you to be more effective in the spirit realm. One of the chief reasons for this is that you can communicate with the angels or any other spiritual being you might encounter in their own language.

As you gain entry into various places in the second and third heaven, you will discover that God does not uncover your eyes to see everything. Notwithstanding, through utilizing your divers tongues, you will be able to detect sounds that will assist you in identifying where you are located. I discovered that certain sounds will come forth from our tongues as a signal to us that there is a demonic presence in the vicinity.

We believe one of the reasons that angels show up with regularity in our prayer times is because of the number of saints who are praying in divers tongues. The angels love intercession, and they also enjoy speaking to those who can converse in their own language about the Heavenly Father and His purposes using divers tongues.

Tongues change as you travel through the various portals and dimensions in the second heavens. I am not completely certain as to why, but this happens with regularity. Some of the tongues may sound more like mysterious sounds than words.

The Numeric Language

While training in this communication center, I started speaking in a numeric language. This was very peculiar and somewhat embarrassing. I felt very foolish praying in divers tongues, and then all of a sudden I am spitting out numbers. There was no apparent pattern to these numbers.

I have consistently been linked to the communication ministry in heaven. In this area, numbers are very vital for initiating systems and executing commands. The fact that the numbers have been spoken primarily in the main communication center in the third heaven and remote communication centers out in the heavenlies suggests to me the numbers are probably encoded messages that the enemy cannot understand. I have heard the enemy speak many languages, but I have yet to hear them speak in a numeric language.

Like the Lord's angels, dark angels speak in numerous languages. However, their speech usually sounds somewhat distorted or perverted with a harsher or rougher tone in their tongues. The exception to this rule is that angels of light sound very similar to the Lord's angels. In fact, it is so close that you really have to be able to discern the minutest presence of evil in order to know you are talking to the enemy.

Up until now, I have not heard many intercessors speak in a numeric language. I am not sure of all the purposes of the numeric tongues. However, through the power of the Holy Spirit, I use them frequently when I am out in the heavenlies. I have found that it plays an instrumental role in unlocking areas, which have coded access points of entry. The Lord has taken me numerous places in the spirit realm where the correct release of numbers opens gates and passageways.

Numbers depict many things. They speak of timing, directions and coordinates in warfare, combinations that unlock doors, even the DNA structure is represented by numbers.

Churches as Communication Centers

I have been highlighting the communication systems of the heavenlies. Why are prayers and intercession so critical? They make up the communication network that links the church with the heavens. Communication centers are being set up all over the world. We know them as prayer centers. However, God is calling on us to step up into a higher level of communication with Him. This is where divers tongues and the angels come in. God is using both to enhance the church's effectiveness in communing with Him and dealing with the enemy. If you do not presently understand and operate in divers tongues, I would highly recommend reading *Divers Tongues* by Ron Crawford[11].

Communications in the Heavenlies

In the coming days, the activities of these communication centers in the church will increase exponentially. Angels will be coming into our churches to ensure the effectiveness of the prayer centers for the kingdom of God. In the spirit realm, the Lord is putting together a network of His churches. There will be times when we will be taken in the spirit to other churches or linked with individuals around the world to intercede with them for the Lord's will to be done. This is already happening in our church.

One of the primary reasons that God is calling us to the heavenly realms is to have us proclaim His purposes in heaven so that they will come to pass here on earth. I recognize that the prayers we proclaim here on earth can have the same end effect. However, if our spirit is speaking from heaven, we bypass the battle of our prayers going heavenward. In addition, when you are praying from heaven your perspective is different and your faith mightier.

Thy kingdom come. Thy will be done in earth, as it is in heaven.
                                             Matthew 6:10

[9] John Bevere, *Under Cover*, (Nashville: Thomas Nelson Publishers, 2001).

[10] Watchman Nee, *Authority and Submission*, (Anaheim: Living Stream Ministry, 1988).

[11] Ronald W. Crawford, Rev. *Divers Tongues: Languages of the Saints*, (Dallas: Pneumatikos Publishing, 2001).

10 Heavenly Training

AS WE continue to explore the heavenlies in the pages that follow, you will see how God desires His children to walk. There will be an unveiling of the supernatural realm in the most extraordinary and unbelievable manner. Our faith will be challenged, as things are not going to continue to go on as usual.

Transportation in the Heavens

In January of 1998 I was taken in the spirit by the Lord to an airport hanger while wide-awake and in intercession. I was looking at the aircraft when unexpectedly I was propelled out into the heavenlies. It was revealed to me later that I had been launched out into the second heaven. When I arrived at my destination, I was completely shocked as before my eyes the

Ministering from Our Heavenly Seats

Lord displayed a heavenly craft. This vehicle looked very similar to what I would have called a spaceship.

I gazed at this heavenly craft for a few moments. At first, I thought my imagination was playing games with me. However, as I viewed this heavenly craft, the Lord quietly whispered in my heart, "This is of Me, don't worry about it."

After I arose from prayer, I was a little bewildered. Quite honestly, I was not convinced that the encounter was of the Lord. I knew the Lord had told me He was in this, but my mind did not want to believe what my spirit had witnessed. Although the Lord was reassuring me with His peace and presence, my religious, analytical mind was kicking into gear. I decided not to relate this encounter to the pastor or my wife for the time being. They both knew I was peculiar, but I did not want them to think I had gone over the edge.

> *For since the beginning of the world men have not heard, nor perceived by the ear, neither hath the eye seen, O God, beside thee, what he hath prepared for him that waiteth for him.*
> *Isaiah 64:4*

> *But as it is written, Eye hath not seen, nor ear heard, neither have entered into the heart of man, the things which God hath prepared for them that love him. But God hath revealed them unto us by his Spirit: for the Spirit searcheth all things, yea, the deep things of God.*
> *1 Corinthians 2:9-10*

A number of days later, while in intercession, I was again taken into the second heaven. Once more, I was shown a heavenly craft. However, this time the Lord placed me inside of the vehicle. As if I was not already freaked out by what was transpiring, without warning the heavenly craft was suddenly launched out into the heavenlies. I gazed on the stars outside the windows and knew I was flying at an unbelievable speed. Since I was in a state of amazement, I was not discerning a great deal and did not notice whether or not there was anyone else on board. My mind was interjecting a lot of questions and doubts such as, "How am I ever going to tell anyone about this?" The Lord encouraged me to calm down. Before I knew it, we had docked at a translucent structure that was solid, yet almost entirely transparent. It had the appearance of a space station. Several of the Lord's angels met me as I made my entrance into the station.

Two days later, I was once again caught up into another heavenly craft. This time the Lord opened my eyes to discover what was inside. There were panels of windows across the top and the sides with an extensive window across the front. In truth, I could view space from about any direction that I turned my head. As we flew, the heavenly craft would spin around several times and without warning shift into hyper-speed. We were traveling on one of the portal highways.

Discerning in the Heavenlies

Before these experiences started, the Lord had me praying on a daily basis for a dramatic increase in my discernment. I had no inkling that the Lord would be putting my discernment to the test at this level. For that matter, I did not even know this level existed!

Ministering from Our Heavenly Seats

I was beginning to discern that there were angels aboard the heavenly craft and that possibly they had been there all along. I constantly pray that the Lord will increase my discernment, but there are circumstances where the Lord does not permit me to discern everything. The ministry of the angels provides an excellent example. There are times when I can tell how many angels are with me, but during the next encounter I will not be sure whether or not they are present. Even though the Lord uses the angels in a multitude of ways, He requires us to look to Him for our needs. God does not want us to depend on His angels for our consolation.

As time went along, I developed a keen awareness that the angels were getting more involved in my training. They were teaching me the technical aspects of flying: what buttons, levers or settings to touch or move in order to fly the heavenly craft. It was also equipped with weapons, and I noticed there were buttons or switches in the armrests that controlled some of the weaponry.

The Lord has not always opened my eyes so I could see clearly. There have been many instances where the Lord required me to perceive or discern what was going on rather than just showing me. We must realize that God wants us to be able to discern with more than just our spiritual eyes. He desires us to utilize all the spiritual sensors with which He has equipped us. We can also smell, taste, feel and hear with our spiritual senses.

> *For now we see through a glass, darkly; but then face to face: now I know in part; but then shall I know even as also I am known.*
> *1 Corinthians 13:12*

Tracking the Enemy

I have trained on many different heavenly crafts and learned from the various crews of angels that were with me. On one particular mission, we were flying in a portal and were scanning for the enemy. We detected a demonic presence, but we were advised by the Lord not to confront it. Instead, we docked at a station maintained by the Lord's angels, which was connected to the main communication center in the third heaven.

I realize that I may be losing a few of you, so I want to interject some thoughts right now. Even the biggest doubters would agree that the enemy appears to know the plans and strategies of the church ahead of time and does everything possible to obstruct them. He hinders our prayers and most assuredly delays the answers. It is glorious how we are starting to disrupt the enemy as he has been disrupting us for so long. Chapter ten of Daniel describes this strategy of Satan's kingdom. Most of the time he knows us better than we know ourselves; and in Ezekiel, we learn why.

> *Behold, thou art wiser than Daniel; there is no secret that they can hide from thee:*
> Ezekiel 28:3

It is from this chapter in Ezekiel that we get much of our information about Lucifer. The enemy realizes the gifts and purposes we possess and tries to exploit them, steal them, or even worse, destroy us. He also has unbelievable knowledge, information, and access to the resources of many heavenly places that fall under the authority of the saints but have been left unoccupied.

Ministering from Our Heavenly Seats

The enemy has access to things that we should be guarding and using. He hinders our prayers, disrupts and destroys God's perfect purpose for people. Why can we not put spies into his camps like Moses and Joshua did to hinder and destroy his purposes? I am tired of getting beat up by the enemy. I am weary of seeing the enemy with such incredible influence on earth. If we are the overcomers that we say we are, let us step into our places in the heavenlies. Jesus restored the dominion influence in which we are supposed to walk. God is revealing to His children during intercession His ways and how to proceed into this dimension of His authority.

> *What is man, that thou art mindful of him? and the son of man, that thou visitest him? For thou hast made him a little lower than the angels, and hast crowned him with glory and honour. Thou madest him to have dominion over the works of thy hands; thou hast put all things under his feet:*
> *Psalm 8:4-6*

> *And Jesus came and spake unto them, saying, All power is given unto me in heaven and in earth. Go ye therefore, and teach all nations, baptizing them in the name of the Father, and of the Son, and of the Holy Ghost: Teaching them to observe all things whatsoever I have commanded you:*

> *and, lo, I am with you alway, even unto the end of the world. Amen.*
> *Matthew 28:18-20*

Encountering the Enemy in the Heavenlies

The gifts God gives us on earth are also to be used in the heavenlies. However, I discovered something very unique about the gift of discernment. In the earthly realm, when an angel is standing near me, I usually feel heat on the side of my face. However, I do not necessarily discern them the same way in the heavenlies. The angels are with me most of the time on these missions. For instance, once I felt heat radiating on the side of my face but knew it was not coming from the presence of a nearby angel. I asked the angel what this meant. He said that the heat I felt on my face was from a scanning device the enemy uses to track us. It is very similar to a laser beam. He also told me the Lord has given us the authority to break off this kind of attack.

What this teaches us is that we need to constantly be tuning in to the Holy Spirit to know what is really going on. The enemy has many ways of disguising his tactics. The Word talks about the *"wiles of the devil"* (Ephesians 6:11). The word "wiles" connotes trickery. The enemy will try to confuse our discernment if he can.

While the enemy craft with the scanning device was positioned in front of us, a dark angel onboard began speaking to me. I want to pause here for a moment and explain more specifically what was happening. What the dark angel was saying from the other craft registered in my spirit. I had never encountered this type of experience before, but I knew the Lord was with me and was guiding me. When this strange communication happened it seemed very natural to me, and I did not hesitate to obey the Lord or even to question Him. I just did it! I have learned to obey the Lord and ask questions later.

Ministering from Our Heavenly Seats

Remember the disciples simply obeying Jesus' command to go get the donkey, or Abraham simply obeying God's command to sacrifice Isaac. Neither of these things made sense in the natural but with God it is better to obey now and ask questions later. If you think about it, this is a powerful principle.

> *Ye shall walk after the LORD your God, and fear him, and keep his commandments, and obey his voice, and ye shall serve him, and cleave unto him.*
>
> *Deuteronomy 13:4*

> *And Samuel said, Hath the LORD as great delight in burnt offerings and sacrifices, as in obeying the voice of the LORD? Behold, to obey is better than sacrifice, and to hearken than the fat of rams.*
>
> *1 Samuel 15:22*

> *Saying unto them, Go into the village over against you, and straightway ye shall find an ass tied, and a colt with her: loose them, and bring them unto me.*
>
> *Matthew 21:2*

> *And he said, Take now thy son, thine only son Isaac, whom thou lovest, and get thee into the land of Moriah; and offer him there for a burnt offering upon one of the mountains which I will tell thee of.*
>
> *Genesis 22:2*

When Christians start realizing that through the Holy Spirit they can accomplish things that are impossible in the natural realm, their spirits are going to soar! God is getting our spirit-man prepared and equipped for the most unimaginable things.

The Lord responded through me in tongues to the dark angel. The next thing I realized was that the Lord had told the angels on board our heavenly craft to destroy this dark angel and his vessel. A thought hit me, "What happens to dark angels when they are destroyed?" The Lord instantly answered my question by saying that when an evil angel is destroyed in spiritual battle, it is immediately cast into hell. These particular dark angels are then "out of the game." They literally have to await their judgment just like dead sinners. In the gospels, when Jesus was delivering the Gadarene man, the demons requested they be cast into the herd of swine. They knew that Jesus could have cast them directly into the abyss as God did to the sons of God in the time of Noah (Jude 6).

I want to clarify this point. There is a difference between dark angels being "defeated" where they can flee and regroup to fight again another day versus times when dark angels are cast into hell and no longer have the ability to roam the earth or the heavens. All judgment is in the sovereign hands of God Almighty and subject to His timing. Just as it is with sinners, God gives the fallen angels the opportunity to obey and flee instead of rebelling and being incarcerated. We do not judge these beings, God does. We cannot determine their fate. God is still merciful to all His creation, even to the fallen angels. We must walk in this same kind of mercy. We cannot indiscriminately attack or declare judgment against the enemy. We must know the mind of the Lord and what He wants us to do.

You might ask, "Why would a dark angel put himself at such risk?" Let me ask you, "Why did a third of the angels in heaven take a gamble in thinking they could rebel against God?" At this point, I can only speculate why fallen angels do the things they do. I do know this, dark angels follow their superiors' orders, usually out of fear, and sometimes out of greed for the "spoils" should they win a spiritual battle.

Preemptive Strikes on the Enemy

Some of the Lord's communication centers in the second heavens have very sophisticated tracking systems. Every enemy craft is plotted and tracked. Words such as "sector" and "quad or quadrant" are used with regularity. In the future, we will be able to use the supernatural information collected by these sights to pinpoint the enemy's main concentration or headquarters in a given area in the heavenlies or down on earth. The enemy and his hosts are tracked meticulously, and God is training His saints to walk in a place of incredible discernment. We will prophetically know the plans and moves of the enemy before he can put them into action. Basically, we can make preemptive strikes on the enemy's kingdom before he is ready. It will be a glorious day of victory for the church when we regularly receive this vital information about Satan's activities.

> *For there is nothing hid, which shall not be manifested; neither was any thing kept secret, but that it should come abroad.*
> *Mark 4:22*

The Lord has had me work through the human mindset that says, "God does everything." God can do anything, but He uses the saints, His angels and yes, even the enemy at times, in order to bring about His purposes. God is omniscient, omnipresent and omnipotent and does not need enemy tracking devices and other instruments. He could accomplish His will all by Himself. God made all creation to work together with Him to fulfill His plan. We have a very simplistic view of how the spirit realm operates, but God is showing more details and giving more understanding of how it operates. Angels are not omniscient. Saints are not all-knowing. God created these devices and systems to allow us to work with Him in the implementation of His plans and purposes. For example, many angels were created to work with these systems. Just like humans, angels have gifts and anointings; furthermore, they have purpose and destiny. While some angels are assigned to sing and worship at God's Throne, other angels are fulfilling their "ministry" with incredible technical skills. These gifts are utilized in the areas I have been describing.

Major Changes Coming to Intercession

One of the questions that I use to ask the Lord is, "Will other saints follow me into the places He has taken me in the heavenlies?" He told me yes. Since then, the Lord has taken several members of our church into some of these heavenly places. A few of them have seen, been in, and even piloted heavenly craft, while others have been taken to communication centers. The Lord has allowed them a taste of what is ahead, but so far they have not received extensive training. Personally, I believe that saints in other churches around the world are already stepping into this dimension of the kingdom of God.

Ministering from Our Heavenly Seats

> *To the intent that now unto the principalities and powers in heavenly places **might be known by the church** the manifold wisdom of God,*
> *Ephesians 3:10*

God will open this revelation to you and your church according to His perfect timing. When He does, this book will provide instruction and affirmation as you see or experience these unusual and exciting dynamics in the spirit realm. These experiences will not be easy to explain to Christians who may be steeped in tradition. Many will quickly conclude that this is a demonic deception. The contents of this book may be taken one of two ways. First, a person will both accept in faith and be obedient to step into these deeper dimensions of what God is asking them to do, or at the very least, support those who are. Second, regretfully, others will completely reject this book as demonic.

Training

Let us move on and discuss more about the training the Lord had me undertake. One day I was placed into the cockpit of a heavenly craft. The best way to describe what happened next would be to relate it to taking a driving test. I was put at the controls and taken through various flying maneuvers that would be impossible for me to perform in the natural. Then I was given specific practice targets at which to shoot. I am very grateful that our spirits can do all the things the Lord asks. If it were left up to my capacities, I would certainly not be able to pass these tests.

Heavenly Training

Suddenly I heard, "step back," and I could hear the angels saying "Here comes Jesus." When Jesus came, His very presence was overwhelming, and I broke into tears. I do not know how to explain the presence of the Lord at this level. He always comes to love and encourage me in what I have accomplished through Him. If it had not been for the Lord's continual involvement, I am not sure I would have been able to get past all the unearthly things He has asked me to do.

In another instance, the Lord sent us on a mission to retrieve three stolen objects from off an enemy ship. The dark angels on board were very agitated and tried to prevent me from taking these items. However, they did not succeed. I took the three items back to our ship and gave them to an angel who took them away. I believe that these three items have prophetic implications that will some day be manifested on earth. The Word tells us that the enemy has stolen from God's people; we are just taking back what rightfully belongs to the kingdom of God.

On another occasion, I was taken in a heavenly craft out into a region of the heavenlies unfamiliar to me. The heavenlies are incredible! I am shown something new every time. Every place you travel has its own features. On this particular day, the Lord Jesus Himself appeared and gave me a very precious gift. You will never have to doubt that the Lord always accompanies you on your missions. He says I will go before you and I will never leave you nor forsake you. He means everywhere, even in the heavenlies.

> *I will go before thee, and make the crooked places straight: I will break in pieces the gates of brass, and cut in sunder the bars of iron:*
> *Isaiah 45:2*

Ministering from Our Heavenly Seats

> *Let your conversation be without covetousness; and be content with such things as ye have: for he hath said, I will never leave thee, nor forsake thee.*
>
> *Hebrews 13:5*

It is not unusual for the Lord to pull you out of what you are doing in the heavenlies and place you at His Throne or in one of His chambers. Many gifts the Lord gives will provide you with distinctly greater power and authority when used here on earth. The gifts and weapons the Lord brings us in the spirit are not always activated or manifested in our lives on earth at that moment but will come to fruition at the proper timing of the Lord. Many have been hidden because they are created for a specific day and hour.

> *And I will give thee the treasures of darkness, and hidden riches of secret places, that thou mayest know that I, the LORD, which call thee by thy name, am the God of Israel.*
>
> *Isaiah 45:3*

> *Every good gift and every perfect gift is from above, and cometh down from the Father of lights, with whom is no variableness, neither shadow of turning.*
>
> *James 1:17*

In *Ministering with Angels*, I talked about the physical manifestations that occurred when we started interacting with angels in the spirit realm. I also said that the shaking and falling over subsided as we ministered with them and became accustomed to their presence. While traveling in a heavenly craft, you may have some physical manifestations as well.

There could be shaking, and there might be the sensation that your spirit is being raptured out of your body. At take off, your spirit may experience a gravitational-type pull from the high speeds at which you are traveling. I have also noticed that when you cross over territorial lines in the heavens, you may experience a certain amount of shaking or vibrating.

There are usually entry points into the various regions of the heavenlies. These places of entrance are called gates. When you enter through a gate, it will register in your spirit in some manner. Now remember, this is how I discern it. The Lord may let you discern it in any way He sees fit, even in a way that is entirely different from mine.

One time we had just entered by way of one of these gates when suddenly there was a dark angel standing in our ship. He had come for something that we had in our possession. We refused to give him what he had come for, directed him to leave and he obeyed. God deposits many things into our spirits; however, the enemy covets and tries to steal what God has bestowed on us. God has placed some extraordinary things within me, some of which I will detail later in this book.

The training in the heavenly craft has varied from time to time. There were instances when I was learning the layout of the controls and how to operate them, while at other times the angels might be sharing prophetic revelations with me. The purpose was about learning God's ways and growing in the Lord, not just about missions and flying.

Obedience is Mandatory

One day during intercession I was placed into a heavenly craft, and suddenly we came upon an enemy ship. You could call it a "word of knowledge" or the "gift of discernment" or whatever you want, but I knew that the enemy occupied the craft in front of us. The gifts God has given you here on earth are also effective out in the heavenlies. I know that in Bible School you do not get textbook examples of how to operate in the gifts of the Spirit in the heavenlies. Nevertheless, the gifts are in operation, and the Lord teaches us how to use them.

As we approached, I could sense the presence of evil resonating from their ship. The Lord told me to not confront them at this time. **It is absolutely essential that we obey the Lord.** God expects His children to use wisdom and be obedient when dealing in the spirit realm, whether on the earth or in the heavenlies. The Lord will not tolerate disobedience at this level of warfare. He will permit mistakes, but not disobedience. King Saul was judged very harshly for disobeying God, and his story teaches us that the greater the authority, the more severe the discipline.

Time to Share the Revelations

For a long time, the Lord would not allow me to share these revelations. When it was His time, the Lord let me know in an unusual way. During one Sunday night service, Pastor Crawford asked me to come to the platform to pray. As I began to pray, the Holy Spirit directed me to address Satan and tell him we were declaring war on his kingdom. While standing before the congregation, my spirit was suddenly transported into the heavenlies and I was flying with angels in a heavenly craft. I really did not know what to do or say, primarily because the Lord had not released me to talk about these things yet.

I continued to pray even though the angels were talking to me, and I could not clearly understand what they were saying. I proclaimed something over our church body and then went back to my seat to contemplate what had transpired. The Lord instructed me that the time to share with the church was approaching, and He would give me the exact timing for the bringing forth of these revelations.

Before I made the revelations public, the Lord gave me an additional confirmation that it was time to share these experiences with our congregation. I was in a heavenly craft and recognized I was with some of our intercessors. This had never happened before. It was an amazing and incredible experience. A few weeks late, one of these intercessors came up to me and shared that they thought they had seen a heavenly craft during intercession on that same night. They had delayed telling me because they were afraid I might think they were crazy. I encouraged them and told them that God was opening up some very unusual things to intercessors and that I would be talking about this in the very near future. I then knew God was confirming that His timing was at hand to share these revelations.

Ministering from Our Heavenly Seats

11 Discernment in the Heavenlies

IN THE early stages of discernment, most people do not see demons or dark angels but rather perceive them. Dark angels from the heavenlies have an incredible ability to cloak themselves. This is because they still reflect and emanate a residue of the glory of the Lord. For this reason, you may not readily perceive the evil in them. This is why it is so crucial that believers step into a higher level of discerning of spirits. Jesus said that deception would come.

> *And Jesus answered and said unto them, Take heed that no man deceive you.*
> *Matthew 24:4*

Angels of Light

> *And no marvel; for Satan himself is transformed into an angel of light. Therefore it is no great thing if his ministers also be transformed as the ministers of righteousness; whose end shall be according to their works.*
>
> *2 Corinthians 11:14-15*

Another name for this kind of evil angel who has the glory of God still radiating from them is "angel of light." There are many angels of light, and they are able to fool most Christians with the presence they bring. Some of the dark angels can appear very attractive (Ezekiel 28:12). Never depend solely on your perceptions, but always apply the scriptural test when dealing with any spirit. Ask them to confess to you that Jesus Christ came in the flesh (1 John 4:1-2).

Several people in our church have encountered these elusive dark angels. Even though these fallen angels can appear beautiful and exude a false love that could be mistaken for the Lord's, you must be careful not to make the mistake of transacting any kingdom business with them. They can appear so pure and radiate a measure of the glory of the Lord, which can be very convincing. If it were not for the Lord's diligence in training us, we would have been fooled very easily.

Please listen to what I am saying. These angels sound like the angels of the Lord. They can speak in the languages of heaven. On the other hand, the languages of many of the lower ranking demons have been perverted and distorted. If there is a danger in ministering with angels, this is it – communing with dark angels! These dark angels will encourage you to worship them. A true saint will not want to worship angels, nor will the Lord's angels give you that opportunity. Why is that? Angels of the Lord will not allow you to worship them!

It is absolutely imperative that we be able *"to discern both good and evil"* (Hebrews 5:14). When God brings you into a greater level of discernment, He will carefully guide you and give you the ability to identify even angels of light. However, it takes humility and an absolute passion to know the Father in order to come into this kind of discernment. Remember that discerning the angels of light is one thing, but having authority over them is another. As we come into an intimate relationship with the Father, the power for overcoming these dark forces will be given as we receive His nature and the authority He wants to invest in us.

Fallen angels who preside in the heavenlies have some unusual powers. Once, I was on a mission and discerned an evil presence coming toward our heavenly craft. All of a sudden, I felt a force hit my stomach area and literally pull and drain my spiritual strength. The Lord had us back off and pull away. Several times on missions for the Lord into the second heavens, I have experienced the enemy literally draining my strength. They possess weapons that can debilitate us, and it is imperative that we are equipped with the proper armor when we do the Lord's bidding in these regions of the spirit realm. We must have the appropriate weaponry to engage these higher-level enemy forces. At the time of this encounter, it could have been that I needed to have greater authority to deal with these beings. I do not know, but let us not forget that wisdom is present to help us know when to and when not to fight. Our first priority is not always to fight but to listen and know the voice of the Lord and discern exactly what He wants done.

Neutral

One evening during a service, a fallen angel appeared to me. Although I had not encountered this dark angel out in the heavenlies, I knew he was highly ranked. He said his name was "Neutral." Throughout this book, I have intentionally not given the names of fallen angels or places in the spirit realm. However, this particular name is very generic and I thought it would help you to remember its purpose and operation.

I did not sense much evil radiating from Neutral. However, I knew immediately that although he called himself Neutral, he was not. The Holy Spirit said that he operates within a fold or slit between dimensions in the spirit realm. Neutral does not readily show himself but stays hidden within this fold as he attacks Christians who have no idea that he is there. Neutral is not easily discerned, and he produces tremendous fruits for his evil labor. This is a spirit the Lord despises greatly because he is neither hot nor cold but is lukewarm. The spiritual influence Neutral exerts creates a complacent and comfortable atmosphere, numbing and corrupting a man's heart without him even knowing it.

So then because thou art lukewarm, and neither cold nor hot, I will spue thee out of my mouth.
                                           Revelation 3:16

Discerning Enemy Ranks

Another excellent example of using discernment in the heavenlies was learned on yet another mission. The Lord asked the crew of our heavenly craft and I to find a specific enemy craft. We searched and eventually found our target. Our sensors showed that there were four dark angels onboard, and I could see two of them in the spirit. One of the Lord's angels told me that one of the four was ranked higher than the other three. This is the authority configuration that often exists on enemy craft.

Those of you who have had a lot of experience in deliverance ministries may see a similarity. When a person is possessed by more than one demon, there is typically a chain of command among those demons. The one in charge usually hides and lets the other demons speak. That is why it is so critical that you locate the highest-ranking demon first and deal with him.

Dark Realm Inspires Hollywood

Many characters depicted on television and in the movies are modeled after dark angels in the heavenlies. For example, while in the heavenlies, I came across a dark being that was dressed similar to Darth Vader, the villain from the Star Wars trilogy. One of the main jobs of this dark angel is to assassinate people or influence humans to kill. Another dark angel I have seen was dressed similar to "Batman." This takes us back to those who astral project. The enemy has allowed many human spirits into realms where they see these beings. In fact, Satan assists many authors, screenwriters, directors and artists to reproduce artistically what he has shown them from the spirit realm. The bottom line is that many superheroes and alien-type characters that are daily put in front of us and our children have demonic roots. I am not telling you to throw away your television or to not go to the movies. What I am saying is that television shows and movies can carry demonic attachments.

Ministering from Our Heavenly Seats

For instance, after watching a popular sci-fi movie, I had a very demonic nightmare that night. The next morning I asked the Lord what caused me to have such a demonic dream. He said the movie provided a breach in the wall for the enemy to enter my home and attack me.

One day while in prayer, I was taken in a heavenly craft to a place farther out in space than I had ever been before. At last, we came to our destination, which appeared to be an enemy stronghold that was some type of space station. Dark angels met us. The Holy Spirit instructed me to talk to them and tell them we had come to take this facility back for the Lord. These dark angels were definitely more alien-like in appearance than others I had encountered. I was ushered by God's angels down a corridor lined with fallen angels. I was told not to look over at the dark angels but to keep my attention straight ahead. We finally came to the one that was in charge. I was there for just a few moments when Jesus unexpectedly appeared. This was the first time that anything like this had happened.

When Jesus showed up, it was absolutely incredible. Everyone's attention immediately focused on Him. At that moment, there came a supernatural confidence in my spirit. I knew that no army, no matter how well equipped, could ever touch our Lord. The fear of the Lord came on the enemy. They knew it was only by the mercy of God that Jesus did not destroy them right then and there.

There was a different demeanor about the Lord in this setting. He was dressed as a mighty warrior, very intimidating. He is the Lion of the Tribe of Judah. This was my first revelation of Jesus as a warrior. I wonder if Jesus looked like this when He visited Joshua outside of Jericho.

Kidnapped

One day I had been taken up into heaven, and the angels were ministering to me. They told me I was receiving a powerful anointing that would affect this church, this city, this country and the world. I could see things being put on my shoulder. The Lord was there, and to my amazement He was singing His purposes over me. It was a glorious and blessed time, which went on for about an hour. All of a sudden, I saw a crocodile in the spirit. The next image I received was the crocodile holding another crocodile in its mouth. These images seemed out of place in comparison to all the things God had been doing up until this point. I did not feel any evil presence; in fact, I still felt the glory of the Lord on me. The next thing I saw in the spirit were eyes looking at me. Although I was not sure to whom they belonged, I knew that I regularly see the eyes of dark angels when they are near.

My uncertainty turned to certainty when I began hearing familiar demonic sounds. It is often a rhythmic clattering sound. I was a little confused by the infusion of these strangely demonic scenes and sounds that were happening while I was in heaven with the Lord. I was not sure what was going on as I had no previous experience from which to draw. I did not know what was happening or what to expect next. This environment made it extremely difficult to discern what was evil and what was of the Lord.

Then, like lightning, I was taken from the glory of the Lord in heaven to a place I did not recognize. It reminded me of one of the heavenly places I had been before. I was dropped down into a holding place, which felt like a hole. There was total darkness, void of any life. I felt completely isolated and alone. If there was a hell away from hell, this was the place. I felt completely forsaken and forgotten. I could not sense even a fragment of the presence of the Lord that only moments ago had riveted me. A dark angel appeared who began threatening me in an attempt to intimidate me. He was doing his best to instill fear in my heart. He told me that God had left me, and I was being taken to the pit of hell. I could feel the evil and sense terror beyond anything you can imagine. Everything happening to me and around me seemed to verify that what he was saying must be true.

One by one, dark angels would come and try to terrorize me. I could sense their hate and disgust. What was absolutely incredible was the peace I could feel deep in my heart. They were not able to cause me to worry or fret. Yes, I was sensing all these evil things happening, but at the same time I knew the Lord was watching over me. I would begin speaking and words of hope would come flowing out of my lips. I was praising the Lord and declaring to the dark angels that God would *"never leave thee, nor forsake thee"* (Hebrews 13:5). Even if they were to take me to the pit of hell, Jesus would be with me. I had been given a supernatural peace that no demonic force could take from me. **I could not feel the Lord's presence, but I had His peace.**

I know you must be wondering why God would allow a "kidnapping" from heaven by dark angels. I will be the first to tell you I had a lot of questions for the Lord about this experience. I do know, like Job, God allowed it for a purpose. Like many of my encounters, this incident provided training for future assignments. I believe that many of my spiritual experiences are prophetic in nature, and I will be involved in similar events in the future here on earth. I knew God was with me; and recognizing that, I knew He had sanctioned whatever was happening.

> *The steps of a good man are ordered by the LORD: and he delighteth in his way.*
> *Psalm 37:23*

> *Yea, though I walk through the valley of the shadow of death, I will fear no evil: for thou art with me; thy rod and thy staff they comfort me.*
> *Psalm 23:4*

> *Though I walk in the midst of trouble, thou wilt revive me: thou shalt stretch forth thine hand against the wrath of mine enemies, and thy right hand shall save me.*
> *Psalm 138:7*

I am learning to not complain about what God allows me to experience here on earth or in the heavens. I also know He always does things very differently than I would.

> *For my thoughts are not your thoughts, neither are your ways my ways, saith the LORD.*
> *Isaiah 55:8*

I learned many lessons from this experience, the most profound one being what it will be like for those who reject Jesus. To die, go to hell and be utterly forsaken by God is indescribably horrific.

> *The Son of man shall send forth his angels, and they shall gather out of his kingdom all things that offend, and them which do iniquity; And*

> *shall cast them into a furnace of fire: there shall be wailing and gnashing of teeth.*
> *Matthew 13:41-42*

I would be amiss if I did not stop and invite any reader who might be reading this book that does not have a relationship with Jesus to come to know Him as Saviour and Lord. It is a very simple, life-changing step to accept Jesus as your personal Saviour. First, the scriptures teach that we are all sinners.

> ***For all have sinned***, *and come short of the glory of God;*
> *Romans 3:23*

> *If we say that we have no sin, we deceive ourselves, and the truth is not in us.*
> *1 John 1:8*

But God loved us anyway and sent a substitute to pay the penalty for our sins. We cannot buy or work our way out of the penalty for sin, which is death. We can only accept the free gift that God offers to us.

> *For God So loved the word that he gave his only begotten Son, that whosoever believeth in him should not perish, but have everlasting life.*
> *John 3:16*

Finally, all we need to do is ask for God's forgiveness and accept Jesus Christ as our Saviour and Lord.

Discernment in the Heavenlies

If we confess our sins, he is faithful and just to forgive our sins, and to cleanse us from all unrighteousness.
1 John 1:9

Please pray this prayer right now.
Dear God in Heaven,
I'm a sinner. I know I need Jesus in my life. The Bible says that Jesus died for my sins at the cross. God, I believe that Jesus died for me, and I believe You raised Him from the grave. The Bible says that whosoever shall call upon the name of the Lord will be saved. Father God, I have sin in my life that separates me from You, and I am so sorry for that sin. I want to be saved. Jesus, come into my heart and take away the burden of sin in my life. I realize that I can do nothing of myself to be close to You. I know that salvation is a gift of grace and only by Jesus and the spirit working in and through me can I obtain salvation. I can never be good enough or work hard enough for this gift. Only through the love and grace of Jesus can I be who God wants me to be. Help me, Lord, to be the person YOU want me to be. Thank you, Jesus. I believe You have saved me.
Amen.

Salvation is a free gift. If you prayed this prayer and meant it, your name is now written in heaven. You are now a part of God's family, and that means you must begin to get to know your Heavenly Father. It is critical that you become an active part of a local congregation of believers as you grow in your new found life. Please contact a pastor near you.

Ministering from Our Heavenly Seats

12 Sending Spies Into the Land

*And Joshua the son of Nun sent out of Shittim two men to spy secretly, saying, **Go view the land**, even Jericho. And they went, and came into an harlot's house, named Rahab, and lodged there.*
Joshua 2:1

ON TWO separate occasions God instructed Moses and then Joshua to send out spies to check out the Promised Land. Many times God sends us out in the spirit to observe what the enemy is doing, both here on earth and in the heavens. In many ways we act as "spies" when we are on these missions. When we are sent in the spirit into the enemy's camp, sometimes we are seen, and on other occasions the Lord hides our presence. The fact is that the enemy is continually doing this himself, trying to gain strategic information on what is transpiring in heaven and what God is doing here on earth. Satan has a multitude of forces busy on a daily basis trying to find ways to hinder or stop God's purposes. The devil also recruits humans to help in his cause. There are many who astral project in and out of places totally unnoticed and not discerned by most Christians. Those involved in ministries of deliverance need to discern for human spirits projecting into their counseling sessions. These spirits come to hinder the deliverance process and to spy out the techniques used in order to defend themselves against being cast out.

Watch Your Mouth

Do not think for a minute that the enemy is not listening in on your conversations. He does this to get information or to discover points of iniquity about which he can accuse you before the Father.

> *And I heard a loud voice saying in heaven, Now is come salvation, and strength, and the kingdom of our God, and the power of his Christ: for the accuser of our brethren is cast down, which accused them before our God day and night.*
> *Revelation 12:10*

The enemy loves to hear us gossiping, criticizing, murmuring or judging one another. He uses our words to fuel his fiery darts. There are several scriptures that teach us to watch our mouths. One of my favorites is:

Sending Spies into the Land

> *Wherefore, my beloved brethren, let every man be swift to hear, **slow to speak**, slow to wrath:*
>
> *James 1:19*

Spies

Why were the spies sent into Canaan? They were finding out the strength of the enemy and what resources were available to them. They also saw the fruit of the land. The fruit can represent the gifts, anointings and authority available to us in our places of inheritance. Although the land had been promised since Abraham, God specifically says His timing for the descendants of Abraham to occupy the land had not come until Joshua's day because the iniquity of the Amorites was not full.

> *But in the fourth generation they shall come hither again: for the iniquity of the Amorites is not yet full.*
>
> *Genesis 15:16*

The enemy in Canaan was ruling from Israel's rightful places of inheritance. The kings of Canaan represent the principalities and powers Paul refers to in Ephesians Six. When it was the Lord's time for Israel to occupy their inheritance, they did not just speak a prophetic word or declare the promise of their inheritance. Israel had to engage in warfare and defeat the current occupants. The enemy did not just leave; they fought to stay in the land. They wanted to continue to enjoy the fruit of the land.

Ministering from Our Heavenly Seats

The enemy tries to stop revelation from coming forth by targeting those whom the Lord has anointed to release His truths. During the days of Elisha's ministry, the King of Syria came to battle against Israel. Although there were many other prophets in Israel, the enemy king only sent his army against Elisha. Why was this? It was because Elisha was regularly receiving revelation about the plans of the enemy and revealing them to God's people, thereby thwarting evil at every turn (2 Kings 6:8-17).

Called to Fight

Many teach that Satan has been completely defeated and has no power to do anything to hurt us. Some contend that we should not be concerned with Satan because God, and only God, must deal with him. The devil has deceived the church down through the ages into believing that he can be defeated with a quick prayer, all the while knowing that this is not the case. Scripture teaches that we are in an all-out fight for which we must give our lives to see His kingdom come.

> *...that ye stand fast in one spirit, with one mind **striving together for the faith** of the gospel; And **in nothing terrified by your adversaries**: which is to them an evident token of perdition, but to you of salvation, and that of God. For unto you it is given in the behalf of Christ, not only to believe on him, but also **to suffer for his sake;***
> *Philippians 1:27b-29*

Those individuals and churches who determine they want to take the narrow road and become what God is calling His children to be will experience some incredible things in the spirit realm. However, they will also become a prime target for the enemy to attack. This is not an easy calling. You will be attacked individually and as a corporate body. It will be a relentless attack. I wish I could tell you differently, but I cannot. The blessings received for stepping into God's perfect purposes far outweigh any struggles you will encounter, and the rewards in eternity are unfathomable.

> *And if children, then heirs; heirs of God, and joint-heirs with Christ; if so be that we suffer with him, that we may be also glorified together. For I reckon **that the sufferings of this present time are not worthy to be compared with the glory which shall be revealed in us**.*
> *Romans 8:17-18*

In order to remove the enemy from occupying our heavenly places of inheritance, we, like Joshua, must fight. I have a collection of books in my library from current day Christian authors who are teaching there is no fighting to be done in the heavenlies. Many teach that we do not need to engage in spiritual warfare. They propose that Jesus did it all and that we just need to sit back and wait. This teaching is not scriptural. Jesus, Paul and John, as well as many other biblical writers, speak about fighting, warfare, weapons and defeating the enemy. Jesus alone paid for our salvation and He attained the ultimate victory. However, we are required to fight alongside the Lord in prayer and intercession.

I am not talking about picking fights or going out and targeting certain principalities and powers, and I certainly do not have a "hit list" of dark angels. There is great importance in staying under covering, submitting to your leaders and not being a "lone ranger." This is imperative to understand. I am talking about churches that have been given specific corporate warfare assignments by God. In these churches, every specific area, the pastoral staff, the leadership, the board of elders, the congregational members are all lined up under the God-established authority in that body in order to accomplish God's purposes in His perfect timing.

Here again, I want to emphasize the fact that at our church our mandate from the Lord is to seek after His heart and to love Him. As we do these things, He is continually revealing to us specific targets, which He assigns to us to take for His kingdom. Even though all the heavenly places legally belong to the Lord, as the body of Christ we have been deficient by allowing the enemy to come and trespass in the places that the Lord has given to us.

God is bringing correction to those teachings, which have misled the church into laying down their swords and believing the lie that God does not want us to fight. We must fight!! It will take a fight for the saints to remove the enemy from the positions they currently occupy in the heavenlies. Members of any church that moves in this level of heavenly warfare will experience enemy attacks, starting from the pastor on down. In Acts 1:8, Jesus said you will be my witnesses. The Greek word for witness in this verse is *"martus,"* from which we get the English word "martyr." In fact, Acts 22:20 and Revelation 17:6 both translate the word as "martyr." Jesus was not just asking us to evangelize with our words but to actually give our lives!! He told us to take up your cross and follow Me. He told His disciples they would drink the same cup of persecution and death that He had.

Sending Spies into the Land

And they said unto him, We can. And Jesus said unto them, **Ye shall indeed drink of the cup that I drink of**; *and with the baptism that I am baptized withal shall ye be baptized:*

Mark 10:39

Ministering from Our Heavenly Seats

13 A Look at Our Enemy

FOR A moment, I want to give you a glimpse of these heavenly seats or thrones from the perspective of the kingdom of darkness. Remember, Satan and the fallen angels were originally created good and then rebelled. Before the rebellion, these angelic beings were gifted in order to fulfill very definite purposes in God's kingdom. After the rebellion, they were just as gifted, and they still had the knowledge and abilities they possessed before their rebellion. In particular, scripture reveals Lucifer's role in God's kingdom before his downfall.

Lucifer, More Than a Worship Leader

*Thou art the anointed cherub that **covereth**; and I have set thee so: thou wast upon the holy*

> *mountain of God; thou hast walked up and down in the midst of the stones of fire.*
> *Ezekiel 28:14*

The Hebrew word for covereth is *"cakak,"* which means "to entwine as a screen, to cover over, protect, defend." Lucifer was not only head of the worship in heaven before he rebelled but was also heavily involved in protecting or providing security for the Throne area. The Lord told me that Lucifer was responsible for security codes and clearances. Why was there a security system needed in heaven? Before the rebellion, the angels had free choice as to whether or not they followed God. God has always protected this very sacred area. Even on earth, great precautions were made for the security of the Ark of the Covenant. I believe Lucifer was also involved in the security system for the portals that transverse all of the Lord's creation. He was a master of the inner workings of the communication and portal systems. We see Satan's kingdom still includes great influence on communications, even Jesus mentions that principality of the dark kingdom known as the Prince of the Power of the Air.

> *Wherein in time past ye walked according to the course of this world, according to the prince of the power of the air, the spirit that now worketh in the children of disobedience:*
> *Ephesians 2:2*

Keys and Codes

While in the heavens, I have traveled through many doors and gates of the spirit realm. As I overcame the enemy at new and higher levels of warfare, I received crowns and anointings. Often the doors and gates in the spirit realm were locked, and it was necessary to have keys or codes to open them. In other words, you need to have the keys or codes to be able to access a particular dimension of the spirit realm.

Sometimes the "key" was something the Lord had attached to my spirit. When the enemy saw the key, they were reluctant but allowed me to gain access. Then there were other times that the "code" was spoken through my tongues as a numeric language. The numbers were spoken in a sequence that unlocked the passageway for me. This has happened on numerous occasions. You cannot just waltz through the spirit realm without the keys and codes, which provide the proper authority. Occasionally, you use these codes without even knowing you have used them.

So likewise ye, when ye shall see all these things, know that it is near, even at the doors.
Matthew 24:33

The keys given are very significant. Some of these keys will unlock the doors of understanding for the end-times; those revelations that were given to prophets of old such as Daniel, revelations that were locked or sealed until the time of the end.

Seventy weeks are determined upon thy people and upon thy holy city, to finish the transgression, and to make an end of sins, and to make reconciliation for iniquity, and to bring in everlasting righteousness, and to seal up the vision and prophecy, and to anoint the most Holy.
Daniel 9:24

Ministering from Our Heavenly Seats

> *But thou, O Daniel, shut up the words, and seal the book, even to the time of the end: many shall run to and fro, and knowledge shall be increased.*
> *Daniel 12:4*

> *And he said, Go thy way, Daniel: for the words are closed up and sealed till the time of the end.*
> *Daniel 12:9*

There are also keys to new doors, which represent new dimensions in God that His children have not yet experienced or entered. We will be absolutely amazed at what we will discover once these doors are unlocked. God is calling His children to drink from one of His deeper wells (Psalm 42:7). He is the fountain of living water and wants us to drink of Him, and not of ourselves.

> *For my people have committed two evils; they have forsaken me the fountain of living waters, and hewed them out cisterns, broken cisterns, that can hold no water.*
> *Jeremiah 2:13*

God's people are going to have dramatic encounters with the Lord that defy description. Be prepared because many of the encounters will be incredibly intense.

As we discussed earlier, many demons have been relegated to the earth. These are the ones that possess and oppress people. On the other hand, dark angels guard the entryways into the regions of the heavenlies that are currently occupied by the kingdom of darkness. I was usually in a heavenly craft when I came to these entry points.

Once the Lord took me into a space station of the enemy where there were coded doors to gain access into vital places. I saw a translucent dark angel stationed at the control panels. His body was outlined in a laser beam, and he was pushing buttons as he monitored the panels with his strange hands and long bony fingers. Red laser beams shot out of the end of his index finger to activate things. The Lord had me address him, and I relayed instructions to him in tongues.

> *To the intent that now unto the principalities and powers in heavenly places might be known by the church the manifold wisdom of God, According to the eternal purpose which he purposed in Christ Jesus our Lord: In whom we have boldness and access with confidence by the faith of him.*
> *Ephesians 3:10-12*

After that I headed across the room to what looked like huge vault doors at a bank. Several of the Lord's angels walked with me up to the door, and I spoke in a numeric language. After the sequences of numbers were spoken, the door opened. The door fanned open in several directions; it did not just swing open. I walked into the room and saw a beam of light shining ahead. We walked up to it. The light was emanating from an opening in the floor. The Lord's angel told me to step down into the lower level through the opening. I stepped down into the lower level, and immediately I realized the beam of light was the glory of the Lord. It was the source of energy needed to operate this space station. I felt very uneasy down in this lower deck, and then I recognized why. I was not alone. Dark angels were down there hiding. I did not respond to their presence. I just got out quickly.

The enemy has nothing that really belongs to him. He uses whatever he can find or steal. The Lord is the source for whatever power he has or utilizes. The enemy steals the blessings that have been set aside for the children of the Lord. We are called to reign in heavenly places in Christ Jesus, but since we have not stepped into our inheritances, the enemy makes use of them (Ephesians 2:6). God is revealing to the church how the enemy operates and is also permitting us to see what the enemy has stolen. God is calling on the saints to take back what the enemy has stolen and to step into their heavenly places in order to make use of the supernatural resources God has provided.

Satan's Thrones

God gave Satan and the other fallen angels a place to live, which is referred to in Jude as their first estate. However, they want more. Actually, they want it all. Through the centuries, they have stolen gifts, anointings and many codes which have allowed them to occupy heavenly places that were reserved for believers. The fall of Adam began the process of Satan taking places that were purposed for God's children to rule and reign over, and this has resulted in a loss of dominion.

Satan's deepest desire is to be worshipped. Throughout the heavenlies, he has captured heavenly thrones, created to offer praise to God, and turned them into places from which he is worshipped. Currently, high-ranking fallen angels occupy many of these thrones of worship. From these thrones, fallen angels engender worship from mankind for themselves or for Satan. They also create havoc here on earth in the territories over which they maintain dominion. Most of these fallen angels stay in these heavenly locations and assign the grunt work of terrorizing humans to lowly demons who live on earth. Many enemy councils are made up of these high-ranking fallen angels that plan the evil strategies of the kingdom of darkness.

> *Hide me from the secret counsel of the wicked;*
> *from the insurrection of the workers of iniquity:*
> *Psalm 64:2*

I have been to a location in the second heavens that operates, in part, as an intercessory ministry empowering Satan. Do not forget that Satan is both limited by and enabled by the laws to which all of God's creation are subject. He understands the law of the power of prayer. The enemy can quote the Lord's Prayer backward and forward. He knows that it says "*thy will be done, in earth as it is in heaven.*" Satan constantly seeks humans to pray for his will to be done. These strategies are birthed in demonic councils in the heavenlies and are prayed for their fulfillment on earth. This is yet another ministry of God that Satan has perverted. Do you know that Satanists even utilize the power of fasting? They fervently fast and pray Satan's will to be done. How much more do we as God's people need to fast and pray for God's will to be done here on earth?

The Bible records examples of this type of intercessory devotion and worship to Satan and the fallen angels.

> *And he brought me into the inner court of the LORD's house, and, behold, at the door of the temple of the LORD, between the porch and the altar, were about five and twenty men, with their backs toward the temple of the LORD, and their faces toward the east; and they **worshipped** the sun toward the east.*
> *Ezekiel 8:16*

Ministering from Our Heavenly Seats

The word "worshipped" in this passage means to "prostrate, bow down or beseech." These twenty-five men were worshipping and praying in the Lord's Temple. They were coming in agreement for the purposes of Satan to be done. Satan does not respect anything that is precious to God. It was not enough that it was a blasphemous act of idolatry, but this was done in the inner court near the manifest presence of God.

Satan's Surveillance Operations

> *And it was told the king of Jericho, saying, Behold, there came men in hither to night of the children of Israel to search out the country.*
> *Joshua 2:2*

Notice here the king of Jericho knew spies from Joshua had come into his city. Never underestimate the ability of the enemy to know what is happening. He is obviously not omniscient; however, he has quite a sophisticated means of communication whereby he carries out his surveillance operations. Even though the enemy may know what is going on, he still does not know the "secret plans" of the Lord. God speaks His mysteries and revelations to His saints with the intention of them waiting for His timing for the release of the revelation. The enemy knows he cannot stop the Lord's purposes, but he can hinder or disrupt them.

Remember, Daniel received revelations from the Lord but was told to seal them up and not declare them at that time.

A Look at Our Enemy

> *But thou, O Daniel, shut up the words, and seal the book, even to the time of the end: many shall run to and fro, and knowledge shall be increased...And I heard, but I understood not: then said I, O my Lord, what shall be the end of these things? And he said, Go thy way, Daniel: for the words are closed up and sealed till the time of the end.*
> *Daniel 12:4, 8-9*

Daniel was told those particular revelations would be opened up in the last days. So it is with the things the Lord entrusts to His saints today. We must listen closely and obey the Lord regarding the right time to release of word from Him. I was instructed of the Lord to wait for several years. I was not to speak of the things I am now sharing with you, before He told me to release them. Even then, the Lord was very specific about when and how I was to speak of the things He had shown to me.

Can the Enemy Affect the Weather?

I learned about the enemy and the weather when I was taken to one of the remote communication centers in the heavenlies. I talked to the Lord's angels at this particular facility. They told me their responsibility was overseeing weather conditions on the earth. This space station functions as a control center for the weather. I saw some of the instrumentation utilized on this space station, and it was extremely high-tech.

This led me to ask the Lord the question, "Can the enemy influence the weather?" That might sound like an

Ministering from Our Heavenly Seats

outrageous question to some, but I think we need to look closely at a couple of scriptures to which the Lord led me.

> *And he arose, and rebuked the wind, and said unto the sea, Peace, be still. And the wind ceased, and there was a great calm.*
> *Mark 4:39*

I think it is very interesting that Jesus "rebuked the wind," but He simply told the sea, "peace, be still." The sea is part of creation and did not need a rebuke, but demonic forces were controlling the wind, and Jesus did rebuke them. The Lord also led me to another familiar passage. This passage is taken from the time when Jesus was walking on the water, and Peter asks if he can come out on the water with Jesus.

> *And he said, Come. And when Peter was come down out of the ship, he walked on the water, to go to Jesus. But when he saw the wind boisterous, he was afraid; and beginning to sink, he cried, saying, Lord, save me.*
> *Matthew 14:29-30*

If I had been the one walking on the water, I think my first concern would have been the water and the probability of drowning. However, notice what brings about the fear that attacks Peter's faith. The wind! The enemy uses the wind to cause fear in Peter's heart and rob him of the faith he had when he first climbed out of the boat and began walking on the water.

A Look at Our Enemy

Who's in Charge?

The dark angels in the second heavens have incredible powers. These powers are far beyond anything the church has ever seen, far beyond the powers of most of the demons currently on the earth. As these fallen angels continue to be pushed out of the heavenly places they have invaded, we can see the eventual all-out war with the enemy drawing nearer.

The fallen angels have tremendous technical skills. They were gifted from the beginning before their rebellion. One area of their expertise is in the sphere of communications. The very name angel means, "messenger," which connotes access to information being obtained and transmitted. Many of these heavenly seats or thrones are spiritual communication centers. When the kingdom of darkness rules from these communication centers, they have access to information, which they use to attack both believers and the church as a whole. When the kingdom of darkness controls portals, they are able to hinder communications between earth and heaven. We see this in Daniel with the Prince of Persia resisting the angelic messenger.

> *Then said he unto me, Fear not, Daniel: for from the first day that thou didst set thine heart to understand, and to chasten thyself before thy God, thy words were heard, and I am come for thy words. But the prince of the kingdom of Persia withstood me one and twenty days: but, lo, Michael, one of the chief princes, came to help me; and I remained there with the kings of Persia.*
>
> *Daniel 10:12-13*

Ministering from Our Heavenly Seats

One of the most important facets of these heavenly places is their relation to the glory of God being manifested on the earth. When the enemy overtakes a heavenly place, he confiscates the glory that God originally intended to flow down to the earth from that place. When saints are positioned in their heavenly seats, they can transact the flow of glory. I have seen places where the enemy rules and also places where saints and angels are ministering.

When the enemy rules, the glory is diverted to power the kingdom of darkness. When saints and angels rule from a heavenly seat, the glory flows down to the earth. In Christian circles, we call it an "open heaven." We hear about churches that through fasting and prayer have an abundance of glory. In those places, the heavenly authority is flowing properly.

The saints need to establish themselves in their appointed seats of rulership. Once there, they can take advantage of the information and glory that is available through that particular heavenly place. Even though we will not know everything about the place from which we are ruling, the information we do get will be extremely helpful. These heavenly places are critical, and the enemy fights to keep them.

What kind of information might we tap into? We can learn the locations of enemy forces on earth and in the heavenlies, which will allow intercessors to target more precisely and defeat more completely specific enemy advances. Remember, weather conditions on earth are tracked from these heavenly places. There will be times when God will allow us to see weather conditions before they occur as a demonstration of His power in signs and wonders.

Scripture speaks of Elijah interceding for rain. He knew from God that when he saw the tiniest cloud, there would be a *"great rain"* (1 Kings 18:44).

In other situations, we will be able to pinpoint weather disturbances caused by the enemy. As I mentioned earlier, there were obviously evil spirits causing the storm on the Sea of Galilee, which Jesus rebuked (Matthew 8:26-27).

We will know where intercession is coming from around the world, so that intercessors can come into agreement globally about the specific purposes of God. Recently, one of our intercessors described a vision in which the Lord took her to a heavenly place and showed her various groups of intercessors around the earth. He had her come into agreement with them in prayer. From our heavenly seats, we will operate with a dramatically more accurate word of knowledge. Without any communication in the natural, we will join other intercessors according to God's direction.

Ministering from Our Heavenly Seats

14 Abiding

Abide in me, and I in you. As the branch cannot bear fruit of itself, except it abide in the vine; no more can ye, except ye abide in me.

John 15:4

OVER THESE last years, the Lord has blessed me with some mind-boggling revelations, but revelation has never been my pursuit. In 1996, when the Lord dramatically touched me, God placed an incredible hunger in my heart for His presence. As a result, I have dedicated my life to interceding for His purposes. If I never receive another revelation, I will still pursue my commitment to pray.

You may be thinking, "Well, that is easy for you to say because you are receiving revelation. It is easy to make commitments to pray for hours a day when you are getting glorious things from the Lord. Would you make the same pledge if you were receiving little or nothing from Him?"

Drastic Changes in Intercession

That is a fair comment. During the summer of 2000, things started changing drastically in my prayer times. Day by day, I began receiving less and less revelation from the Lord. In addition, I was not experiencing the same level of the glory of His presence in my life to which I had become so accustomed. I went from having astounding encounters with God at His Throne to wondering where He had gone.

Naturally, my first reaction was to look inwardly, searching to see whether I had done anything that caused God to pull back from me. This was a very painful test. The enemy came with great force to convince me that I had lost favor with God and that He was rejecting me.

At this juncture, I began asking the Lord questions like, "Is this a sign that I do not need to pray as much?" What made matters worse was that my senior pastor did not seem to be having the same experience. In fact, he seemed to be flourishing spiritually. I found myself struggling with jealousy and rejection. I felt very forsaken.

There were many occasions when I wondered if I should leave this particular church body. I wondered if my ministry at Lakewood was concluding. However, the Lord kept telling me that everything was fine and that I was being taken through a time of transition. Even hearing these assuring words that were clearly spoken by the Lord did not resolve the turmoil within me.

I did not get angry with God, but I did get very frustrated. I was now going for weeks without really hearing from Him. I cannot begin to describe the desperation I was experiencing. Going to pray became a complete act of faith. At this point, I had to believe that even without the fireworks that had been so typical of my prayer times, God was listening and was still going to use me. He had promised many marvelous things for my life and ministry, but I seemed to be going in the opposite direction from where I thought I should. I asked the Lord, "Should I not be receiving dreams and visions? Should I not be getting more prophetic words? How am I to be the leader You called me to be, if I cannot hear You telling me anything?" With all the frustration and discouragement, I finally told God, "I give up!"

That is when God very quietly and gently began speaking to me again. His voice was now a "still small" voice, not the thundering "you would have to be deaf to not understand what He is saying" voice. He told me He had not forsaken me. In fact, He had answered my heart's prayer. I thought, "Do what? You answered my heart's prayer?" Then He asked me, "Did you not pray and say that you wanted to have a passionate heart for Me and an incredible desire to live in My presence? For you to see these things come to pass in your life, you have to die." However harsh I had perceived God to be during this dry time, I now saw His hand and purpose clearly.

Timely Reading

At different times during this season, God brought timely books into my life. However, I must caution you about reading books. Like anything else, it can be taken to an extreme. We can find ourselves spending more time trying to learn how to experience God than praying and seeking for intimacy with Him. Let God lead you to read the books at His appointed times. On the other hand, do not let being too busy to read be your excuse either. Most of us can trim some time off our TV viewing and read instead.

There were four authors that God especially used to influence my walk with Him. They are Francis Fenelon, Madame Guyon, Andrew Murray and Watchman Nee. All of these great saints had an incredible walk with God, and have gone on to be with our Lord. As you study their lives, you can see a common thread that links them all together. They all learned how to abide in Christ. I realized this was the critical lesson God was trying to teach me. As you read about these individuals, you will learn that it will take a lifetime commitment of pressing in to God to truly abide in the Lord.

If I had to pick one book out of the many these authors produced, it would probably be Fenelon's, *The Seeking Heart*[12]. Even though this book was written several hundred years ago, the message ignites a passion in your heart for intimacy with God. I would also highly recommend Madame Guyon's biography. This book can be a great encouragement for those who are going hard after the Lord, but their spouse is not. Be warned, though. These books will not offer easy or quick solutions. Basically, they will help you learn how to die to self.

Abiding

Please understand, to come to a place of abiding requires the relinquishment of every facet of your life. I am still very young in this process, and I find God continually shining His light on areas in my life that require removal with His divine knife.

> *Every branch in me that beareth not fruit he taketh away: and every branch that beareth fruit, he **purgeth** it, that it may bring forth more fruit.*
> *John 15:2*

I do not want to paint a negative picture. It is not that abiding in Christ is difficult. It is not, but it does require that you give up your life for His.

His Chambers

I have had the privilege of seeing many things in heaven and throughout the spirit realm. Yet, there is absolutely nothing that compares to the intimate times when the Lord calls you to Himself. There are times when He meets with you in His chambers, and you know that you have His complete attention. In these treasured moments, He lets you know how much He loves you, and how pleased He is with what you are doing. The Lord never condemns or harps on our many mistakes and shortcomings. Instead, He is always building us up and drawing us closer into His heart.

What I have found very interesting is the timing of these intimate encounters. Often a visitation such as this will come right after a season of ferocious warfare in which I have taken a step of faith done on God's behalf in the spirit realm. However, encounters with the Lord can happen at any time. He loves to surprise us with a visit.

One thing that occurs pretty regularly when the Lord visits me is a shortness of breath. His presence literally takes my breath away. It is very similar to the sensation of hyperventilating. There may be times when your physical body will start shaking uncontrollably. Obviously, your encounters will be personally tailored by the Lord and could be completely different from mine. However, there will be something very special about each of His visitations. An encounter with the Lord feels very different than a visit by an angel.

John 15

Any real study of abiding in the Lord will lead you to John 15. This special chapter is where the Lord led me and has had me return again and again. My life and everything I do filters through the lessons I have learned in John 15. In this powerful chapter we learn how both Jesus and the Father are involved in making sure we abide in them.

I am the true vine, and my Father is the husbandman.
John 15:1

The Holy Spirit also gets involved. That fact is revealed in chapter 14.

Abiding

> *And I will pray the Father, and he shall give you another Comforter, that he may abide with you for ever;*
> *John 14:16*

So basically, you have the entire Trinity working in tandem to make sure your abiding will be a success.

Many people think that abiding in the Lord would begin at the point of salvation. Unfortunately, most of the time, this is not the case. Paul the Apostle realized that the process of abiding was a daily act of dying.

> *I am crucified with Christ: nevertheless I live; yet not I, but Christ liveth in me: and the life which I now live in the flesh I live by the faith of the Son of God, who loved me, and gave himself for me.*
> *Galatians 2:20*

The abiding comes as we die to our self-nature or the soulish realm. As I have said, it is a process, and it begins and ends with God. The work continues until we go home to be with Christ.

> *Being confident of this very thing, that he which hath begun a good work in you will perform it until the day of Jesus Christ:*
> *Philippians 1:6*

It might be helpful if I described what kind of life I led before I began abiding in the Lord. I would become very frustrated with myself at times because of the inconsistency of my spiritual walk. I would be doing very well, and then some circumstance would hit my life and I would start sinking. I might spiral for a few days, weeks or even months. I would often pray or even make a fresh commitment to the Lord but that did not always pull me out of my despair. All I wanted was to have the peace and presence of God restored back into my life. The problem was that I used my own efforts to try to get my spirit back in line.

It is at this very juncture that we must give up and allow God to do the work that only He can do. All of us know that our salvation is by grace and through faith alone. There are absolutely no works we can do that will place us in right standing with God. It is through the blood of Christ that we are saved, and it is purely by His righteousness that we can come before the Father. The point being, we have nothing to do with making salvation work; we are only the benefactors.

Sanctification Takes a Lifetime

Given what I have said about salvation, what about sanctification? Sanctification is a work of faith as well. We have to daily place our lives in God's divine hands and allow Him total control. We must trust Him even when the things He allows in our lives are not pretty, fun or pleasant. We cannot step out of the process and expect it to be completed. We have to learn each lesson and pass each test or we do the lesson over until we pass that test. Sanctification is the process where most believers stop. They want salvation but they do not want to step into the process of sanctification. Salvation is instantaneous, but sanctification takes a lifetime of dying to our self-nature. It is the process that God uses to make us more like His Son, Jesus Christ our Lord.

Abiding

This brings us back to abiding. If we do not abide in Him, we will not experience the full scope of what God wants to accomplish in our lives. As you see, sanctification and abiding go hand in hand.

Why Discipleship Fails

Many churches have discipleship programs where they teach new converts how to live for God. More often than not, the discipleship process involves memorizing scriptures, learning important stories in the Bible and how to share your testimony. We keep these disciples busy learning facts about God. We teach them scriptures and works, but we do not teach them to develop a relationship with the Living God or how to live a life of abiding in Him. Ultimately, these new believers live lives tied down to religious laws and traditions and believe that is all they need to do to please to God. Most young disciples live in constant condemnation because they discover that despite all their efforts, they cannot "keep clean." They get frustrated and say, "What is the use!"

> *And thou shalt love the Lord thy God with all thy heart, and with all thy soul, and with all thy mind, and with all thy strength: this is the first commandment.*
> *Mark 12:30*

Many churches put their young disciples to work when they should be teaching them to pray, love the Lord and pursue a relationship with Him. So much more valuable work is done for the kingdom of God when our Heavenly Father or the Lord Jesus directs our efforts instead of following the wisdom of man.

> *Because the foolishness of God is wiser than men;*
> *and the weakness of God is stronger than men.*
> *1 Corinthians 1:25*

Another frightening consequence is that young disciples may pattern their walk with the Lord after the shallow spiritual life-style of most modern believers. This is truly a scary scenario. What will these young believers see at their local church? At some churches, they will discover a country club-like atmosphere. There will be lots of talk about sports, school, kids, work, and everything else but the Lord. Some congregations are filled with cliques, which makes it hard for a young believer to find acceptance in the church.

In some churches, new believers observe the faithfulness of the older generation of Christians and find that attending the weekly service is definitely optional. In fact, they soon learn that family activities take precedent over God's plans for the day. Basically, young believers observe lukewarm Christians and do their best to emulate them and adopt their lifestyles in living for Christ.

Who does the Pastor Serve?

We can readily see the results of new converts following in the footsteps of the traditional churchgoer. Would these young believers find a better pattern to follow in the pastors and leaders of their church? Unfortunately, the pastors and their associates are often too busy serving their congregations. They are constantly having meetings and attending conferences in order to glean ideas on how to more effectively serve their congregations and improve church attendance. Many pastors are

Abiding

worn out or burned out. Our churches are full of people who must be served! They are full of pastors who are doing everything except what God really wants of them. He has called the pastors and placed them in the church to serve the Lord. Their job is to abide in the Lord and to find out what God's purposes are for His people. Tragically, if the pastors attempt to do what God really wants, which is to pray, worship and study the Word, the people gripe because the pastor is not catering to their needs.

> *If my people, which are called by my name, shall humble themselves, and pray, and seek my face, and turn from their wicked ways; then will I hear from heaven, and will forgive their sin, and will heal their land.*
>
> *2 Chronicles 7:14*

If there is anyone who needs to be abiding in the Lord, it is the pastors. It is truly a shame that the demands of many congregations discourage their pastors from spending time alone with God. It is imperative for the church to wake up and start abiding in Christ. Many churches are now at risk of missing out on what God desires for them to do in their communities and cities. If pastors and churches do not tune in quickly, they are going to miss their end-time instructions.

As I look across America, in general, my greatest concern is that the church is in danger of missing God's perfect purposes. If the church does not wake up soon, I foresee God saving the lost, teaching them how to abide and turning the work that is to be done over to them. I hope and pray that I am wrong, but I see only a remnant of the modern day church getting on board with God's plans and purposes. How many more revivals will He have to send to America for us to honestly wake up?

Most of the church world does not even see the need for abiding. Those who do realize they need to abide in the Lord think that their own efforts will produce an abiding in the Lord.

> *I am the vine, ye are the branches: He that abideth in me, and I in him, the same bringeth forth much fruit: for without me ye can do nothing.*
> *John 15:5*

Faith's Part in Abiding

We must put our faith in our Father that He will help us to stay connected to the vine. Faith is ceasing from all our efforts and dependence on anyone or anything else, but the Lord. Faith is telling God you are helpless without His help. Faith is putting our lives into His hands to do the work He has promised to do. You cannot abide in the Lord on your own efforts. One of the crucial things to remember is that God must be the One in charge of your development, not you. This is known as the school of the Lord, and you need to enroll. We must stop worrying about getting our lives together by our own efforts and allow the Husbandman to do His work.

> *In that day sing ye unto her, A vineyard of red wine. I the LORD do keep it; I will water it every moment: lest any hurt it, I will keep it night and day.*
> *Isaiah 27:2-3*

You might ask, is it possible to abide in the Lord 24 hours a day, seven days a week? According to the passage above, if we were to do the work of abiding, the answer would be no. However, if we allow God to do the work, it will certainly be possible. How can someone do two things at once? That was my struggle. How do I do the work of the day and at the same time keep my mind on the Lord? Here again, if the burden is on me to make it happen, it will not work.

I know this goes against everything we are taught. We are taught to give 110% of our effort. As Americans, we pride ourselves on being independent and accomplishing our goals with our own talent and savvy. We are recognized and rewarded for our hard earned successes. We like to translate that work ethic to following Christ. Unfortunately, it does not work.

Does God Know You?

The Lord is not looking for our wonderful ideas. He is not looking for someone who will work for Him by burning the midnight oil. He is not grading us on how many people we see healed or even how many souls we lead to Christ. What is the Lord looking for? How strong our relationship is with Him. "Does He know us?" is the great question.

> *And then will I profess unto them, **I never knew you**: depart from me, ye that work iniquity.*
> *Matthew 7:23*

Our abiding in Him is crucial for our existence as a believer. If you are frustrated and seem to be spinning your wheels, ask yourself, or better yet, ask God, "Am I abiding in You? Do you know me?"

When you are abiding in the Lord, there is a supernatural peace that your heart experiences. There is nothing like knowing you are only doing what God wants done. There is nothing like knowing that your motives will not interfere because they are surrendered to God.

The abiding process is simple. Thank the Lord that we do not have to stop everything we are doing in order to be able to abide in Christ. By faith, we trust that the Lord is right there with us, even when other things occupy our minds. We can learn to have the rest, peace and joy in spite of the fact that we have to live in a hectic and sometimes chaotic world.

Even if we are able to get past the hindrances of our mind and not worry if it is always focused on God, we soon learn there are other obstacles to our abiding in Christ. One thing that keeps us from the abiding process is our assumption that perfect fellowship with Christ is only attainable if we do not sin. All of us continue to fail in one way or another, but the Lord wants to abide with us even though we are not sinless.

> *But the Lord is faithful, who shall stablish you, and keep you from evil.*
> *2 Thessalonians 3:3*

> *But the God of all grace, who hath called us unto his eternal glory by Christ Jesus, after that ye have suffered a while, make you perfect, stablish, strengthen, settle you.*
> *1 Peter 5:10*

Here again, we see that it is not by our own efforts that we can keep from sin, rather it is God who will establish and keep us from sin. We must realize that it is Christ's righteousness that God looks at when we come to Him, not ours.

A Word from Jesus

During prayer one day, Jesus came to talk with me. I sensed so much love and acceptance from Him. He told me:

"I allow your spirit to get so thirsty because it brings forth things in your soul that need to be dealt with. In essence, the absence of sensing My presence around you all the time creates a pure desire for it in your spirit, but it also brings out the carnal nature of your soul, such things as jealousy, envy and suspicion. These evil influences try to make their way into your life when you are at the desperation state of wanting to know My Presence.

Do not take on burdens and responsibilities unnecessarily. You cannot force abiding on others. It has to be lived. You can tell others how wonderful it is but do not demand that they do it. I do not demand it. I long for you and others to abide in Me, but it must come from a heart that loves and desires Me, not from one who thinks they have no choice. If the people want and desire with all their heart to have this kind of intimacy and walk with Me, they can have it. There is not a blueprint for how each individual comes to the place of abiding in Me. You cannot dictate how it will come about in their life; they will have to trust Me. It means greater sacrifice for some than for others. For some, it might mean facing the death of someone very dear to them. James, Stephen and even I myself were very dear to many believers. For some, it may mean giving up family and friends. For others, it means walking away from lucrative jobs or rewarding careers.

There is no cost to you for your salvation. I paid for that. However, there is a cost for our friendship. *It is allowing* *the refining process to take place, whatever that may be and not rebelling against it. My ways are not your ways, so you cannot expect anything to be predictable. It is easy to become rebellious in the process because you want instant results. Learning to abide will take a lifetime. Do not try to take shortcuts, just know it is done at My pace and in My way. Learning to abide will cause your heart and mind to be transformed. You will find that where you once had ought against someone, you now have an incredible love for them. Life will no longer be drudgery; instead it will be a delight in spite of all the difficult circumstances you may encounter. In the midst of all of this, do not forget that obedience is paramount. **If you do not obey, you will not abide.***"

> *And the king said unto Araunah, Nay; but I will surely buy it of thee at a price: **neither will I offer burnt offerings unto the LORD my God of that which doth cost me nothing**. So David bought the threshingfloor and the oxen for fifty shekels of silver.*
>
> *2 Samuel 24:24*

> *Then said Jesus unto his disciples, If any man will come after me**, let him deny himself, and take up his cross, and follow me***.
>
> *Matthew 16:24*

---

[12] Francis Fenelon, <u>The Seeking Heart</u>, (Jacksonville: The SeedSowers, 1992).

15 Shaking of the Heavens

Prophetic Shaking

ONE OF the unique things that occurs during my intercession is that my body shakes. This shaking began early in 1997 and continues today. There are times when it becomes very intense. I asked the Lord why I shake while I pray, and He told me that it was prophetic. I believe that in part it is indicative of the specific intercession the Lord has me involved in with the future shaking of the heavens.

> *Mine heart within me is broken because of the prophets;* ***all my bones shake****; I am like a drunken man, and like a man whom wine hath overcome, because of the LORD, and because of the words of his holiness.*
> *Jeremiah 23:9*

At Least Two Shakings

In the Word, we are told about at least two separate shakings that will take place. There is the shaking that is mentioned in Hebrews which I believe refers to the church, and there is the shaking referenced in Matthew and Revelation which describe the battle that takes place in the heavens when Satan and the other dark angels are defeated and cast to the earth.

> *Whose voice then shook the earth: but now he hath promised, saying, Yet once more I **shake not the earth only, but also heaven**. And this word, Yet once more, signifieth the removing of those things that are shaken, as of things that are made, that those things which cannot be shaken may remain. Wherefore we receiving a kingdom which cannot be moved, let us have grace, whereby we may serve God acceptably with reverence and godly fear: For our God is a consuming fire.*
>
> Hebrews 12:26-29

> *Immediately after the tribulation of those days shall the sun be darkened, and the moon shall not give her light, and the stars shall fall from heaven, and the **powers of the heavens shall be shaken**:*
>
> Matthew 24:29

> *And there was **war in heaven**: Michael and his angels fought against the dragon; and the dragon fought and his angels,*
>
> Revelation 12:7

Shaking of the Heavens

*And I heard a loud voice saying in heaven, Now is come salvation, and strength, and the kingdom of our God, and the power of his Christ: for the accuser of our brethren is **cast down**, which accused them before our God day and night.*
Revelation 12:10

The Initial Shaking

Some historians have suggested that the Book of Hebrews was written in A.D. 69 before the destruction in A.D. 70 of Jerusalem and the Temple. They believe that when the writer of Hebrews speaks of the shaking of the earth, he is most likely referencing the final destruction of the Temple or Judaism. In A.D. 70, Jerusalem was destroyed, and the Jews were scattered. As of yet, the Temple has still not been rebuilt. Jesus foretold the destruction of the Temple as a final physical proof that His blood cleanses us from sin and that the blood of sacrificial animals was no longer acceptable before the altar of God. In these last days, God will shake everything on the earth and in the heavens, including everything in the church that is "made," meaning formulated by men, so that those eternal things which cannot be shaken will remain.

Even though the destruction of the Temple was tragic, what is crucial for us to understand today is what is to be shaken from the heavenly side. The heavens represent Christianity. This shaking will affect the church across the whole earth. It is a shaking that will affect everything that man has placed into the church. "*As things that are made.*" Every doctrine, theology, tradition, program, organization, committee, etc. will be subjected to the shaking of God.

Ministering from Our Heavenly Seats

The Lord says the shaking will remove everything that has been made by man so that only the eternal or spiritual things remain. We would like to think that God is wholeheartedly interested in what we make for Him on earth. However, His concentration is on establishing His kingdom on this earth.

> *Wherefore we receiving a kingdom which cannot be moved, let us have grace, whereby we may serve God acceptably with reverence and godly fear:*
>
> *Hebrews 12:28*

His priorities often run contrary to the priorities of most churches today. God wants to build our churches on spiritual foundations. He wants to conduct heavenly business in our sanctuaries, and for that matter, in our cities. He is looking for a people who want to know Him by the Spirit. The churches that are built upon a spiritual structure will survive the upcoming shaking.

> *He is like a man which built an house, and digged deep, and laid the foundation on a rock: and when the flood arose, the stream beat vehemently upon that house, and could not shake it: for it was founded upon a rock.*
>
> *Luke 6:48*

All that really matters is the spiritual church, the body of Christ. It is invisible to the natural eye. The incredible buildings and ministries we have built have very little value to the Kingdom because they are not spiritual in nature. **Is it more advantageous that we provide comfortable seating for our congregations, or would it be more useful to teach them to discern the spiritual gates within our sanctuaries from which**

they can access the heavenlies? Is it more important to have our people fill the various seats on committees in our churches, or is it more imperative to encourage our people to step into their seats on spiritual councils in Heaven? Can we honestly say that there is more going on within the kingdom of God in our churches than there is in the natural?

When God shakes the general church, the only thing left will be what He has established. The only thing standing will be the spiritual foundations He has laid. It is only what God builds spiritually that has any eternal value. The question that every church must ask is, "What have we been building?" If the earthly shaking was so devastating that the Temple and Jerusalem were destroyed and the Jews scattered without a homeland for almost 2000 years, what can the church expect when it is shaken?

The Holy Spirit was sent both to birth and administrate the church. Unfortunately, man has tried to take over His job. Most of us have become hard workers for the kingdom of God. Many great things have been done on behalf of God, many with the purest of motives, but by and large these things have been done by our own efforts. Most of our efforts are centered on decisions and resources that have been supplied at the earthly level. However, the Apostle Paul presents a very clear picture of where our supply source and knowledge should originate.

> *Which he wrought in Christ, when he raised him from the dead, and set him at his own right hand in the heavenly places, Far above all principality, and power, and might, and dominion, and every name that is named, not only in this world, but also in that which is to come: And hath put all things under his feet, and gave*

> *him to be the head over all things to the church,*
> *Ephesians 1:20-22*

> *And hath raised us up together, and made us sit together in heavenly places in Christ Jesus:*
> *Ephesians 2:6*

> *If ye then be risen with Christ, seek those things which are above, where Christ sitteth on the right hand of God. Set your affection on things above, not on things on the earth.*
> *Colossians 3:1-2*

Every church as well as every individual believer should revolve around what is happening in Heaven. Scripture says that our affections should be centered above, not on the earth. If we are ever to sit in heavenly places, our focus will have to change. Our affections must turn from what our congregations need to what God wants. It all has to do with knowing God and dwelling in His presence in Heaven.

The Laodicean church was known for being lukewarm. We are also aware that their condition repulsed God.

> *And unto the angel of the church of the Laodiceans write; These things saith the Amen, the faithful and true witness, the beginning of the creation of God;* ***I know thy works****, that thou art neither cold nor hot: I would thou wert cold or hot. So then because* ***thou art lukewarm****, and neither cold nor hot,* ***I will spue thee out of my mouth****. Because thou sayest, I am rich, and increased with goods, and have need of nothing; and knowest not that thou art wretched, and*

Shaking of the Heavens

> *miserable, and poor, and blind, and naked: I counsel thee to buy of me gold tried in the fire, that thou mayest be rich; and white raiment, that thou mayest be clothed, and that the shame of thy nakedness do not appear; and anoint thine eyes with eyesalve, that thou mayest see. As many as I love, I rebuke and chasten: be zealous therefore, and repent.* ***Behold, I stand at the door, and knock: if any man hear my voice, and open the door, I will come in to him, and will sup with him, and he with me.*** *To him that overcometh will I grant to sit with me in my throne, even as I also overcame, and am set down with my Father in his throne. He that hath an ear, let him hear what the Spirit saith unto the churches.*
>
> Revelation 3:14-22

God said He knew about their works, but the tragedy was that He did not know them. The Lord goes on to tell them that they needed to have their eyes anointed. Why? I believe it was because He wanted them to be able to see the spiritual realms. In this same passage, God also encourages them to abide in Him. He tells them that He is knocking at the door wanting them to come and sup with Him. The Father loves to have His children around His Throne. God wants to have an intimate relationship with all of us. He wants us to be close to Him so that He can share with us the concerns of His heart.

The Final Shaking

There is another shaking that is spoken of in the Bible.

Ministering from Our Heavenly Seats

> *Immediately after the tribulation of those days shall the sun be darkened, and the moon shall not give her light, and the stars shall fall from heaven, and the powers of the heavens shall be shaken:*
> *Matthew 24:29*

Mark and Luke also reference this same end-time event (Mark 13:25; Luke 21:26). While the first shaking mentioned involves the eternal church and will affect the earthly church, this latter shaking will occur in the second heavens. As part of this shaking, Revelation 12 says that the archangel Michael will expel Satan and his angels from the heavens.

> *And I heard a loud voice saying in heaven, Now is come salvation, and strength, and the kingdom of our God, and the power of his Christ: for the accuser of our brethren is cast down, which accused them before our God day and night.*
> *Revelation 12:10*

> *And there was war in heaven: Michael and his angels fought against the dragon; and the dragon fought and his angels,*
> *Revelation 12:7*

I pray that the revelations I have shared will help shed light on the kinds of things that are going on in these realms. The enemy has been occupying many heavenly places for quite some time. The saints have been called to partner in clearing these areas of enemy forces. I also believe that with the kind of training God is giving the saints, we will be used in the war when Michael leads the heavenly hosts against Satan.

Shaking of the Heavens

The shaking in the heavens will be progressive. There will be battles to rid the enemy from places, which lie outside his first estate, and then there will be the final war in the heavens when Satan and the dark angels are cast out of the heavens permanently.

There has been a move by the Lord to begin the first stage of the heavenly shaking. As I have related in this book, we are starting to take back places in the heavens that belong to the Lord but have been unoccupied by the saints. God is calling us to the battle. Although there are plenty of skeptics on this subject, God is revealing the battles that are ahead for us in the heavenlies to many intercessors and prophets.

You may be thinking, "If I am raptured up to heaven, why would I be involved in a battle during the last days?" Always remember that God does everything through intercession. When we are in the spirit, we are not constrained by time but are in the eternal realm. Therefore, we may experience many of the things in the spirit before they are manifested on earth.

God Wants to Lead His Children

God has always wanted man to depend upon Him. Unfortunately, it seems that man has always been determined to live his life on this earth depending on his own resourcefulness. Repeatedly, throughout the Bible we see men and women have to come to dire straights before they realize that they cannot do this thing alone.

Ministering from Our Heavenly Seats

Moses came to the realization that he could not lead the nation of Israel without the help of God. In fact, he told God that he was not going to go forward unless God promised to go with him.

> *Now therefore, I pray thee, if I have found grace in thy sight, shew me now thy way, that I may know thee, that I may find grace in thy sight: and consider that this nation is thy people. And he said, My presence shall go with thee, and I will give thee rest. And he said unto him, If thy presence go not with me, carry us not up hence.*
> *Exodus 33:13-15*

Ultimately, God wants to lead us individually and corporately as His people.

> *Then a cloud covered the tent of the congregation, and the glory of the Lord filled the tabernacle. And Moses was not able to enter into the tent of the congregation, because the cloud abode thereon, and the glory of the Lord filled the tabernacle. And when the cloud was taken up from over the tabernacle, the children of Israel went onward in all their journeys: But if the cloud were not taken up, then they journeyed not till the day that it was taken up. For the cloud of the Lord was upon the tabernacle by day, and fire was on it by night, in the sight of all the house of Israel, throughout all their journeys.*
> *Exodus 40:34-38*

In the above passage, we discover that the children of Israel moved only as God directed. The supernatural manifestation of God let them know when and where they were to go. However, even with the spectacular signs and wonders of God present, the people's hearts eventually hardened. By the time of Samuel, Israel had rejected God as their king and leader.

> *Then all the elders of Israel gathered themselves together, and came to Samuel unto Ramah, And said unto him, Behold, thou art old, and thy sons walk not in thy ways: now make us a king to judge us like all the nations. But the thing displeased Samuel, when they said, Give us a king to judge us. And Samuel prayed unto the Lord. And the Lord said unto Samuel, Hearken unto the voice of the people in all that they say unto thee: for they have not rejected thee, but they have rejected me, that I should not reign over them.*
> *1 Samuel 8:4-7*

God Wants to Lead His Church

Before Jesus ascended to Heaven, He promised His followers that He would send the Holy Spirit to help them. The Lord told them to wait for the Holy Spirit.

> *And, being assembled together with them, commanded them that they should not depart from Jerusalem, but **wait** for the promise of the Father, which, saith he, ye have heard of me.*
> *Acts 1:4*

Ministering from Our Heavenly Seats

Most of us are not good at waiting. The group Jesus was talking to started out with 500 and ended up with 120, which lets us know that waiting was not their strong suit either. The church was born on the day of Pentecost and experienced phenomenal growth. We see from the very genesis of the church that the Holy Spirit plays a pivotal role in it. The early church leaders were always careful to consult the Holy Spirit in the various decisions they made.

God Sets a Pattern

Throughout history God has given specific directions and commands only to later because of the hardened hearts of the people, have them compromised. In the early church there were many patterns established which God intended us to follow. Similar to the children of Israel, the current church has strayed away from patterns God established. We must return to the principles that were instituted in Acts and other New Testament books in order to find out where we erred. In our study, let us remember that God's ways can be discovered by searching out concrete examples and following His commands.

The chronicles of the beginnings of Christianity can be found in Acts. In Acts 11, Luke relates that believers in Christ were first called Christians in Antioch.

> *And when he had found him, he brought him unto Antioch. And it came to pass, that a whole year they assembled themselves with the church, and taught much people. And the disciples were called Christians first in Antioch.*
> *Acts 11:26*

The things that happen in and around the church in Antioch are very critical in discovering God's pattern for churches today. In Antioch, we see one of many patterns the Holy Spirit established in the early church.

> *Now there were in the church that was at Antioch certain prophets and teachers; as Barnabas, and Simeon that was called Niger, and Lucius of Cyrene, and Manaen, which had been brought up with Herod the tetrarch, and Saul. As they ministered to the Lord, and fasted,* **the Holy Ghost said,** *Separate me Barnabas and Saul for the work whereunto I have called them.*
> Acts 13:1-2

In the decisions we make as churches, we should follow the pattern of Barnabas and Paul. These men were spiritually gifted enough that they could have launched their own ministries. Thankfully, they did not head out on their own but were humble enough to rely on the Lord to let them know the timing and to what places they were to travel. They did not receive their directives from men or an organization, rather through the guidance of the Holy Spirit.

Before we become involved in any kind of ministry, we must be sure the Lord has initiated it or else it is in the flesh. The generally-accepted philosophy is that God is looking for volunteers. However, the truth is that whether individually or corporately as churches, we have a very specific purpose that we were created to perform. These purposes are determined by God and can only be revealed by the Holy Spirit. The work is His, and He will touch the hearts of men to do His work. No matter how good our intentions may be, our efforts cannot take the place of divine initiative. God has graciously given us patterns which, if followed, will enhance our decision-making. The call of Paul and Barnabas was individual, but the sending forth was by the corporate body. The pattern I desire for all of us to understand is that Paul and Barnabas were sent forth at the request of the Holy Spirit.

How do most churches function today? Most churches are directed by the decisions of their pastors and leaders. If the pastor is evangelistic or missionary minded, then the church will flow in that direction. If the church has a heritage of having a great choir and music program, then you can expect many performances. The point is most of the time a church will do what it has done for 25 years, or they will take on the ministry emphasis of their current pastor.

When was the last time a church had a prophetic presbytery to find out what God wants them to do? He may want to do something dramatically different from what has been done in the past. In fact, He may want a church to do something that the majority of the congregation does not want to do. Most of the time, we come up with good ideas and programs and then ask God to approve them. Does this follow the New Testament pattern?

Revival, Reformation Or Revolution?

What needs to happen in the churches in America and across the world is for them to hear what God wants to do. Many say we need major revival to hit America. God has already sent some major outpourings of His Spirit all over our country. I do not think revivals are the answer.

I would like to define what revival, reformation and revolution are and then have us consider which one would have the greatest affect on today's church.

Revival – a renewed attention or interest in something, a period of renewed religious interest.

Reformation – to put or change into an improved form or condition, to amend or improve by change of form or removal of faults or abuses, to be changed for the better.

Revolution – a sudden, radical, or complete change, a fundamental change in political organization: the overthrow of one government or rule and the substitution of another by the governed, fundamental change in the way of thinking: a change of paradigm.

Revival calls for a renewed interest in God and reformation calls for improved state of the individual or church in general. However, a revolution calls for a "sudden, radical, or complete change" in the individual or church. I like that!!

There is no way that churches in America or the believers within them will ever get to where God wants them to be with just revivals or even with reformation. God is calling for a revolution within the body of Christ. He wants to give our churches a thorough purging so that they can once again be fruitful. Our world cannot survive the continued pervasiveness of the enemy in almost every aspect of our lives. Nor can our world call on the current church to help lift it from the stranglehold the enemy has on it at this present time.

I do not mean to be pessimistic, but we do not stand a chance without God stepping in and rescuing us. He will do this when we humble ourselves and pray. However, it will take a drastic revolution in our walk with God if we are to see the necessary changes. God is grieved by the way we drink from His holy river of refreshing, only to go back to what we were doing before.

God Administers the Local Church

God wants His church to come into agreement with His kingdom purposes. At the present time this is impossible because His church is divided. Paul rebukes the Corinthians for being divisive. He said they were guilty of separating themselves, "*I am of Paul; and I of Apollos; and I of Cephas; and **I of Christ***" (1 Corinthians 1:12). Interestingly, one of the definitions given in the English dictionary for "sect" is a religious denomination. In Paul's list of the works of the flesh in Galatians 5, he mentions **"heresies."** When you look up heresies in *Strong's Concordance*, it is used interchangeably with the word **sect**. If the Holy Spirit did not want sects in the church, then why do we have denominations?

God will visit many churches to see if they are willing to forsake all and become united in the body of Christ. Most churches operate within denominations and organizations, which were established on particular doctrines. The Apostle Paul spoke adamantly against any group breaking off from the body of Christ. Paul said that even if one was basing their departure from the church on following Christ, it was even unscriptural.

As spiritual leaders, we must be seeking the Father for what He wants done in our churches. We have addressed the fact that, in general, most churches have diverted from the biblical pattern the Holy Spirit established. Only by prayer and fasting will a church and its leaders find the answers and guidance from the Holy Spirit to align with the Father's heart.

The things I have shared in this book give only a glimpse of what is taking place in the kingdom of God. God is on the move in the heavens. He desires for us to partner with Him in removing the enemy from places he is not intended to be. God wants us to do many things on His behalf in order to take dominion of this earth. To find out what our responsibility is in this huge undertaking, we must be in a position to hear what the Father is saying.

The heavens are being affected by our intercession. God is taking us into places and showing us things that are incredible. The shaking of the heavens has begun. For you to know what is going on and what you are to do, you must know the Lord in a way far beyond what you have ever known.

These are glorious days for the church! These are also days of serious decisions. What will you do in response to what God is speaking to your heart right now? The Lord loves you and wants to draw you into Himself and show you the things to come. Your choice to partner with God comes with a great cost. Namely, you will have to forsake all to follow Him.

Ministering from Our Heavenly Seats

RECOMMENDED READING

Books for Saints

Divers Tongues   **By Ronald W. Crawford**

The author, a seasoned pastor, takes us through God's Word as he unveils the strategic communication tool of divers tongues. This long hidden and misunderstood gifting brings spiritual warfare victories that are both wondrous and compelling.

Hierarchy   **By Ronald W. Crawford**

The realm of the spirit operates according to a precise structure of authority. Clearly depicted in the Bible, this organizational pattern is implemented within the Kingdom of God and the kingdom of the enemy. Doctrines of devils and the traditions of religion have kept these principles hidden, and the church has suffered as a result. The author unveils the Biblical patterns of authority that govern heaven and earth, as well as the release of power that flows from them. A must read for intercessors and those engaged in spiritual warfare.

Pneumatikos   **By Ronald W. Crawford**

As Priests of the Most High, the Pneumatikos minister before the very Throne of God. It is their privilege to communicate the secrets of the Kingdom to a church that is hungry for more of God. These spiritual ones are the Kings and Priests of the Book of Revelation, and will proclaim the mysteries of God to this world.

Princes   **By Ronald W. Crawford**

Our enemy is Satan, but he does not fight alone. The Bible directly identifies many evil rulers with which the church must contend, each with very specific tactics and purpose within the kingdom of darkness. The author describes several of these beings from the vantage point of the Word of God, as well as from direct encounters with them. Let us not be ignorant of any of the devices of our enemies.

Seers Catalog   **By Ronald W. Crawford**

God is awakening the office of the Seer. The Spirit of God is revealing many things in these days to those whose ears and eyes are opened. Learning how to utilize your senses will serve you in knowing how to be a proper steward of the mysteries of God.

The Saints   **By Ronald W. Crawford**

Jesus is rising with His Saints to conduct the battle of the end times. The forces of righteousness are being called and commissioned at this time. The King of Saints is searching for people who will follow Him in battle. Discover how to be one of God's mighty men and prepare for war!

Ministering with Angels   **By Paul David Harrison**

One of the distinguishing characteristics of the culminating events in God's timetable will be the influx of the angelic in our churches and individual lives. They are coming at God's bidding to impart gifts and anointings reserved for these last days. (Also available in Spanish)

Ministering from our Heavenly Seats   **By Paul David Harrison**

Scripture says God has "...made us sit together in heavenly places in Christ Jesus." The author describes what it is really like to pray and minister from the seats of authority God has purposed and prepared for His Son's bride, the church.

Topical Studies for Saints

Dreams & Visions   **By Ronald W. Crawford**

The missing gifts of Pentecost are those which allow for communication with the most High at all times of the day and night. Consider the meaning and power of dreams and visions as they are detailed in the Word of God. They are as much a part of the promise of the Father as is unknown tongues.

Fighting the Good Fight   **By Ronald W. Crawford**

We are at war! The key to victory is not found in our weapons, but in our attitudes. God will grant to us triumph as we grant to Him our perceptions.

Manual of Five-Fold Interpretation   By Ronald W. Crawford

God desires to communicate with His church today! One of the ways in which this specific word from God will be conveyed and interpreted is through these five comprehensive offices: apostle, prophet, teachers, evangelist and pastor.

Proskuneo   By Ronald W. Crawford

The posture of prayer for the time in which we live is clearly stated within the Word of the Lord. The Bible clearly tells us that in heaven and on earth we must lay all that we are before Him in prayer.

Right Hand and Left Hand   By Ronald W. Crawford

A collection of sermons concerning the right and left in scripture. God has much to say regarding this vital insight, and He intends for you to know it. A grasp of the essential truth of relationship and acquisition could mean the difference between blessing and defeat in your life.

Selah   By Ronald W. Crawford

Throughout the writings of David, the concept of Selah is mentioned over seventy times. This powerful word indicates much more than a pause for reflection. Selah is that juncture that connects the promises of God with their fulfillment. Selah is the manner in which God causes His children to step into their heritage of blessing and power. We must understand and embrace the Selah if we are to move within the Tabernacle of David.

Seven Thunders Revealed   By Ronald W. Crawford

The Word of God tells us exactly how His children are to move within the authority of His heavenly Throne. A very clear progression of four stages of power is depicted within the Book of Revelation. God will use this mighty principle of righteous rule to change the planet. This understanding is a must for anyone that desires to be used of God in these last days..

Sprinkling of the Blood   By Ronald W. Crawford

The Blood of Christ is essential in the process of salvation, but our need for the blood does not end at the inception of the Christian life. There is a blood sprinkling that is readily declared in the New Covenant, and we must utilize this sprinkling in order to move progressively forward into the deeper things of God.

Stork Women of Shinar   By Ronald W. Crawford

What is located in the place of ancient Babylon? What is the identity of the feminine spirits that have taken the ephah of wickedness to this ancient place? How do we overcome them for the cause of righteousness?

The Timing of God   By Ronald W. Crawford

Timing is vital in all that we do, whether in the natural or spiritual realm. When we grasp the importance of the timing of God, we will position ourselves for miracles.

His Kingdom Come   **By Paul David Harrison**

The missing element of the gospel message is as Jesus prayed, "His kingdom come." This study presents how absolutely essential it is to preach about the kingdom of God including the Biblical precedent for preaching about angels and the things of the spiritual realm.

Saints' Network Authors

Breaking Chains of Darkness   **By Charles Baker, PhD.**

The author explains the tactics of the enemy in establishing strongholds in Christians and how they can be ended by the power of the Blood of Jesus.

School of the Saints   **By Mark Burke**

Many Christians have been drinking milk too long. God is releasing fresh manna and meat from heaven, opening the eyes of understanding and training His saints for these last days. Will you enroll in God's school of the saints?

Training of a Saint   **By Mark Burke**

We must ask the Father to open our spirits to receive the deep truths of His kingdom. We need the anointings of God to understand and comprehend all that He is currently saying to His church. We must be trained to be people who grasp what the Lord is doing, the saints.

Preparing His Own   **By Dennis Stewart**

This three-volume series is a practical review of Jesus' teachings to His twelve disciples during the beginning, middle and end of His ministry. The book's simple premise is to discover all you can about what Jesus wanted His disciples to know and in the process you will discover what Jesus wants you to know.

The City Taking Anointing   **By David Wright**

Covenant is the basis of our Lord's redemptive process. It is time for you to understand and appropriate powerful covenant principles such as the creational covenant of worship and the everlasting covenant, to transform your city into the place of its destiny in the coming glory of the Lord.

PNEUMATIKOS PUBLISHING
P.O. Box 595351, Dallas, Texas 75359
(214) 821-5290 fax (214) 821-0670
www.pneumatikos.com or email info@pneumatikos.com